T0358250

Cambridge Elements ≡

Elements in Environmental Humanities
edited by
Louise Westling
University of Oregon
Serenella Iovino
University of North Carolina at Chapel Hill
Timo Maran
University of Tartu

NONHUMAN SUBJECTS

An Ecology of Earth-Beings

Federico Luisetti
University of St. Gallen

Shaftesbury Road, Cambridge CB2 8EA, United Kingdom

One Liberty Plaza, 20th Floor, New York, NY 10006, USA

477 Williamstown Road, Port Melbourne, VIC 3207, Australia

314–321, 3rd Floor, Plot 3, Splendor Forum, Jasola District Centre, New Delhi – 110025, India

103 Penang Road, #05–06/07, Visioncrest Commercial, Singapore 238467

Cambridge University Press is part of Cambridge University Press & Assessment, a department of the University of Cambridge.

We share the University's mission to contribute to society through the pursuit of education, learning and research at the highest international levels of excellence.

www.cambridge.org
Information on this title: www.cambridge.org/9781009475969

DOI: 10.1017/9781009442770

First published 2023

A catalogue record for this publication is available from the British Library

ISBN 978-1-009-47596-9 Hardback
ISBN 978-1-009-44278-7 Paperback
ISSN 2632-3125 (online)
ISSN 2632-3117 (print)

Nonhuman Subjects

An Ecology of Earth-Beings

Elements in Environmental Humanities

DOI: 10.1017/9781009442770
First published online: November 2023

Federico Luisetti
University of St. Gallen

Author for correspondence: Federico Luisetti, federico.luisetti@unisg.ch

Abstract: The surging wave of Indigenous politics, rights of nature, and social movements acting with rocks, rivers, glaciers, and lakes has brought to light an ecology of nonlife. Its protagonists are "earth-beings," geobodies that question deep-seated Western notions of personhood. Mountains in the Andes, erratic boulders, a landfill in the Swiss Alps, the sacred stones of the Standing Rock Sioux Reservation, and the works of contemporary artists who have engaged with nonlife reveal the subjectivity of beings that are not sentient and alive as biological organisms.

Keywords: environmental humanities, decolonial ecology, political ecology, political geology, rights of nature

ISBNs: 9781009475969 (HB), 9781009442787 (PB), 9781009442770 (OC)
ISSNs: 2632-3125 (online), 2632-3117 (print)

Contents

... / I am a stone / in me / the history of the world.

Galindo (2017, 198)

[P]olitics is primarily conflict over the existence of a common stage and over the existence and status of those present on it.

Rancière (1999, 26)

1 Crisis of Presence

1.1 Farewell to the Holocene

On the road that leads from Potenza to Matera, around ten kilometers after the turn off for Tricarico, there is a minor road that branches off and descends toward the Basento Valley. Leaving behind Castelmezzano Murge on the left – bare beaches of gravel, inaccessible eagle and vulture nests – the road reaches the village of Albano. A magical life that is still intense and widespread engages the seven hundred families of this village.

(De Martino 2015, 55)

The anthropologist Ernesto De Martino and collaborators, who were in search of traces of ancient practices of magic, visited Albano di Lucania, a poverty-stricken rural area in the southern Italian region of Basilicata, between May 17 and May 28, 1957. There, they collected ethnographic observations and tape-recorded interviews documenting the survival of an "archaic regime of existence" (De Martino 2015, 85): magic spells and bindings, possessions, exorcisms, hallucinations, paroxysmal explosions, helping spirits, second personalities. De Martino interprets this "intense magic life" as the manifestation of a collapse of individual forms of personhood, a true psychosocial "crisis of presence" caused by "the collapse of the sheer possibility of making itself the center of decisions and choices according to values" (98).

Afflicted for centuries by an endless chain of social traumas and environmental disasters, oppressed by usury, famine, and plague, the peasants of Lucania could not perceive themselves as centers of "realistically-oriented" actions and decisions and include their lives in the "modern sense of the world" of post-Enlightenment Europe (De Martino 2015, 188). "The precariousness of life's elementary goods, the uncertainty of prospects for the future, the pressure exercised on individuals by uncontrollable natural and social forces" (85) established a "horizon of the crisis," a condition marked by the "frailness of presence" and the constant experience of "being-acted-upon" (15). For De Martino, the "uninterrupted pressure of uncontrollable forces" and the impossibility of "realistic, efficacious behaviors for dealing with the negative and bringing it down to a human proportion" (178) created the peculiar mental formations of this rural population, a unique constellation of nonmodern subjectivities.

My thesis is that the implosion of the sense of reality and individuality captured by De Martino in post-World War II Italy has now escalated into a geohistorical dimension: climate change and the environmental catastrophe have caused a crisis of presence of planetary proportions, which is reframing the experience of being a subject in the age of global ecological disruption. The fundamental categories that have structured the horizon of human action are now shaken by other-than-human existents "with whom we share a common condition: the 'terrestrial condition'" (Gosselin & gé Bartoli 2022, 15). Since Charles David Keeling measured with precision the atmospheric concentrations of carbon dioxide at the Mauna Loa Observatory in Hawaii in the 1960s, proving the anthropogenic origin of climate change, an existential and socio-ecological breakdown of presence has infused our inhabitation of the Earth. The frailness felt by the peasants of Lucania is now spreading in the guise of psychopathologies of environmental vulnerability.[1] Nature has lost its innocence: we look at the clouds and we think of extreme weather events; we eat and we envision intensive animal farming and monocultures.[2]

In the new millennium, the notion of the Anthropocene has popularized this sense of being-acted-upon by uncontrollable environmental forces. Greenhouse gas emissions and the exploitation of natural resources have altered the Earth's metabolism, with gloomy consequences: "we are still largely treading on *terra incognita*," warned Paul Crutzen in his seminal essay "Geology of Mankind" (Crutzen 2002, 23). Ice-cores drilled in ancient ice sheets in Antarctica, Greenland, and nonpolar glaciers have revealed 800,000 years of climatic past and inscribed the short span of human history into the threatening deep time of geohistory (Burgio & Guaraldo 2022). The popularity of the Anthropocene thesis coincides with the compelling scientific revelation that the concentration of carbon dioxide has surpassed 400 parts per million, almost twice the amount that characterized the Holocene's interglacial period of climatic equilibrium. A 12,000-year ecological niche, which allowed humans to become protagonists of natural history, has come to an end; the biosphere has entered a perilous "New Climate Regime" (Latour 2017).[3] The extreme environmental conditions that our human ancestors experienced during the Pleistocene are returning, accompanied by unprecedented evolutionary pressures.

---

[1] Psychological disorders now include "solastalgia," the homesickness for a missing comfortable environment, and "eco-anxiety," the anticipated loss of a habitable future (Clayton 2020).

[2] Environmental historians have shown how ecological concerns about deforestation, desertification, soil depletion, and climate change have accompanied colonial expansion since the early sixteenth century (Anker 2001; Grove 1997).

[3] On the debate concerning the proposed starting date of the Anthropocene, see Lewis & Maslin (2015).

Earth system scientists have reacted to the crisis of presence triggered by climate change by placing the Anthropos at the center of the environmental crisis and by treating humanity as a "species being," a precarious biosocial subject enmeshed in a planetary system of out-of-joint feedback loops and at risk of extinction (Chakrabarty 2009; Colebrook 2014).[4] However, voices from decolonial and Indigenous studies, environmental history, political ecology, the environmental humanities, and ecofeminism have changed the terms of the conversation (Barca 2020; Bonneuil & Fressoz 2016; Mbembe 2019). In this Element, I rely on their counternarratives, which make visible the historical origins of the environmental crisis of presence. The farewell to the Holocene is not the beginning of the "age of Man" (the Anthropocene). It is a reminder that we have been living for five centuries in the age of Capital (the "Capitalocene," Moore 2016), plantations (the "Plantationocene," Ferdinand 2022; Haraway 2016), and wasting relations (the "Wasteocene," Armiero 2021). Humans were not acting as a species being when they enslaved other men and women of African descent, massacred Indigenous people, and destroyed environments across four continents. They accomplished their designs as European white male colonists, rentiers, and metropolitan business elites. Racialized and subaltern people have not asked to be aggregated into a fuzzy biosocial Anthropos and held collectively accountable for climate meltdown and the pillage of ecosystems. The Anthropos is a fictional subject, an obfuscation of colonialism, class, race, and gender relations.

With respect to the civilizational subterfuge and historical short-sightedness of the Anthropocene thesis, decolonial ecologies have objected that the planetary dislocation of personhood began in the "long sixteenth century," with the transatlantic slave trade and the early commodity frontiers of European conquest (Mignolo 2021; Moore 2000). The hold of the slave ship, rather than the cotton gins and steam engines of the Industrial Revolution, is the matrix of global environmental havoc. Today's monoculture farming of wheat, corn, soybeans, cotton, mushrooms, eucalyptus trees, and countless other crops and trees is prolonging the plantation system established with sugarcane and African slaves across the tropics, a "colonial inhabitation" that is still characterizing the global environment (Ferdinand 2022). From the very beginning, plantations were nature factories, a cornerstone of the biological imperialism of

---

[4] Systems ecologies model the Earth as an immense cybernetic organism, in which material and energy flows regulate the mineral and ecological cycles of the biosphere (Odum & Odum 2000). Within this paradigm, inorganic matter is just a component of the "life-support system" of living beings and humanity, the laboring slave of life. According to Yuk Hui, cybernetics has become the lingua franca of Earth system sciences and the Anthropocene's managerial ecologies because ecology is, from its foundation, "a cybernetic concept" (Hui 2019, 39).

European colonists and financers (Crosby 2004). People, plants, and animals were eradicated from their socioecological contexts, transported across the globe, and assembled as forced labor in the inhuman laboratories of New World plantations (Hopes & Perry 2019). The unprecedented flows of materials and labor put in place by this circulation of natures have carved on the planet an immense rift between colonies and metropolitan centers, disrupting humanities and territories (Martinez-Alier 2010). Environmental conflicts about waste management, land and water appropriation, biodiversity conservation, mineral ores, fossil fuels, renewable resources, and biomass are spreading across the planet, reproducing this original colonial fracture.[5] And neoliberal ecologies are globalizing these injured environments through cybernetic modelings of life-support systems, marketizations, deregulations, and speculative objects of trade (abstract emissions units, ecosystem services, carbon markets) (Dehm 2018).

The crisis of presence unsettling the planet is sustained by this perverse coordination of environments in the Global North and the Global South, an articulation that produces new subjects: in the Global North citizens are asked to interiorize green guilt, embrace net-zero lifestyles, and orient their choices toward decarbonization (Aronoff et al. 2019), whereas in the Global South mining, land grabs, and contamination are the rule, creating disposable lives sacrificed to resource extraction (Gómez-Barris 2017; Lerner 2012; Mezzadra & Neilson 2019). When Indigenous people are not expelled or persuaded by corruptive practices to leave room for new plantations, mines, and energy infrastructures (Verweijen & Dunlap 2021), they join world markets under the stewardship of transnational non-governmental organizations (NGOs), becoming "ecological natives," guardians of biodiversity (Ulloa 2017; Watson et al. 2020). As I will argue in the following pages, this ecocidal "regime of planetarity" (Bonneuil 2020) is challenged by multispecies approaches, which express the growing opposition to the capitalist globalization of nature and the imagination of livable alternative worlds. Multispecies thinking is a creative koine animated by mutualist and symbiotic biologies, relational and pluriversal ontologies, posthumanism, intersectional approaches, ecosemiotics, and epistemologies of multinaturalism, trans-corporeality, intra-action, and living entanglements. It battles the neoliberal hegemony by appealing to cooperative interpretations of evolutionary principles.

And yet, multispecies thinking is often centered on life, a biocentric notion that cannot fully acknowledge the modes of existence of abiotic formations, other-than-human geobodies whose timescales and modes of existence defy the

---

[5] See the conflicts documented by the Environmental Justice Atlas (https://ejatlas.org/) and the Manifesto from the Peoples of the South: For an Ecosocial Energy Transition (https://pactoeco socialdelsur.com/manifesto-for-an-ecosocial-energy-transition-from-the-peoples-of-the-south/).

coordinates of living beings.[6] In the next sections, I expound a central argument: beyond neoliberal and multispecies ecologies, the surging wave of Indigenous politics and ecosocial movements acting and thinking with mountains, subsoil, air, and waterbodies has brought to light a "third ecology," an ecology of nonlife. Its protagonists are nonbiological subjects that resist the neoliberal globalization of nature. Activists and communities worldwide are fighting against the theft of natural resources and the loss of livelihoods (Martinez-Alier 2002; Peet & Watts 2004; Sassen 2013). Their engagement is reconfiguring the boundaries that separate what is subjective, valuable, and social from what is disposable, objectual, and exchangeable. Rocks, ice, water, and air are now perceived as ecological, legal, and political subjects, the most vulnerable beings in the neoliberal planet. Emerging multispecies people (mountain-people, river-people, desert-people) ask that we rethink the terrestrial condition from the perspective of subjects that are not persons or alive, as organisms are (Gosselin & gé Bartoli 2022, 209). These beings belong to a relational field, but their eccentric subjectivity troubles biocentric conceptions of life and personhood. They disclose subjective worlds within the planetary world, removed from the history of life.

The current ecological crisis brings us back to Johann Wolfgang von Goethe's experience of the incommensurability of nonlife (Goethe 2016). Imagining himself on the top of "a barren peak," surveying the valleys below, nonlithic nature appears to Goethe as a "perpetual grave" (913). The mountain granite is instead "before" and "above all life," a "primal world" of peaks that "have never given birth to a living being and have never devoured a living being" (913). In tune with a "long tradition of mining the philosophical from the lithic" (Cohen 2015, 4), I reflect on stones and other nonbiological beings to sketch out a decolonial ecopolitics of nonlife. Earth-beings – a term borrowed from Marisol de la Cadena's ethnography of Andean Indigenous politics (de la Cadena 2015) – are geobodies that question the spell of Western biocentrism and challenge deep-seated notions of life and personhood.

After World War II, De Martino witnessed with fascination the "pathological experience of being-acted-upon" by socioecological forces of dispossession (De Martino 2015, 97). He documented peasants' attempts to counter the collapse of individual presence, and reflected on the creative forms of existence

---

[6] Geobody is a term derived from geological modeling of seismic events and geologic features. It has also been used as a critical tool to unpack the colonial construction of space through surveys and cartographical representations (Winichakul 1994). D'Avignon (2020) extends its application to the "human-spirit pacts" in which claims to mineral resources and the subsoil are inseparable from ancient ritualized mining practices. We should not mistake geobodies for "hyperobjects" (Morton 2013). What matters in the case of geobodies is not their scale or perceptual evidence but their political ontology.

elicited by subjection. Now that the environmental crisis of presence is redesigning life and nonlife at a planetary scale, nurturing unparalleled alliances of humans and other-than-humans, we can reflect on the emergent forms of subjectivity. In this Element, the reader will encounter geobodies – rocks, valleys, rivers – exposed to immense forces of commodification and extraction, and I will suggest that we familiarize ourselves with the temperament of glacial erratic boulders, a hidden landfill, and the "sacred stones" of the Standing Rock Sioux Reservation. In dialogue with these earth-beings and with works by artists that have engaged nonlife – Julian Charrière, Regina José Galindo, Giuseppe Penone, and Motoyuki Shitamichi – I will show how the neoliberal globalization of nature is confronted by beings whose political subjectivity cannot be modeled on Western notions of personhood.

Thinking and acting with earth-beings requires a third ecology, an alternative "imaginary for a politics of reality" (de la Cadena & Blaser 2018, 5), the awareness that geobodies are subjects in their own way. Otherwise, if their other-than-human existences are subsumed under the all-encompassing regime of biological life, how could they enter democratic compositions with plants and animals, including the human animal? Unless earth-beings are framed as subjective nonlife, the multispecies insurgence against neoliberalism will exclude what does not comply with the normative universe of the living. If we do not envision just alliances with geobodies, they will appear to us only as monsters, as "morphological divergences" that evoke a confused curiosity or a radical fear of the inanimate (Canguilhem 2008, 134–6).[7] In this Element, I will share what I learned from Andean rocks, Alpine erratic boulders, and North American stones: the principles of a decolonial ecology of nonliving subjects.[8]

1.2 Neoliberal and Multispecies Ecologies

Let me clarify how I understand neoliberal and multispecies ecologies. To the existing ecological crisis, neoliberalism has added its own ruthless "creative destructions" (Harvey 2007): hundreds of structural adjustment programs imposed by the World Bank and the International Monetary Fund in the Global South have crushed customary rights, communal practices, sustainable local economies, and democratic ecologies. Privatization, deregulation, and

---

[7] Here, I betray Georges Canguilhem's biocentric thought and apply his notion of monstrosity to nonorganic natures: "We must reserve the qualification 'monster' for organic beings. There are no mineral monsters" (Canguilhem 2008, 135).

[8] There are several examples in research and activist contexts of becoming subjective in rock, ice, water, and airbodies. Among them, see the Ex-Snia Lake in Rome (https://lagoexsnia.wordpress.com/) and the Embassy of the North Sea (www.embassyofthenorthsea.com/).

financialization of water, forests, soil, and minerals have dispossessed local inhabitants and empowered transnational corporations.[9] The urgent need to address climate change and the loss of biodiversity has deepened neoliberal management of the biosphere and accelerated the efforts to integrate financial and human capital into the two-headed monster of "natural capital" (Prugh et al. 1995). Green New Deals announcing energy transitions and low-carbon infra-structures are slowly under way on both sides of the Atlantic.[10] Through carbon markets and ecosystem services, neoliberalism has inserted capital in the past, present, and future of the land, sea, and atmosphere (Lele et al. 2013; Lohmann 2016; Wainwright & Mann 2018). Humans and other-than-humans have become knots in natural capital's metabolism, resources and casualties of what I call a "neoliberal state of nature" (Luisetti 2019). This neoliberal consensus has colonized knowledge production and international organizations, dictating recipes for economic and environmental globalization (Dardot & Laval 2014).[11]

Capitalism has responded to the environmental crisis of presence with a toolbox of net-zero standards, voluntary reductions of emissions, carbon trading, and the speculative accounting of sustainability, a flexible governance that strives to combine the management of ecosystems with marketization and dispossession. These policies rest on a neoliberal epistemology that has dis-mantled the opposition of nature and society through a malicious interpretation of evolutionary history. Friedrich Hayek prescribes that social scientists, pol-icymakers, and economists rely on "adaptation to the unforeseeable," strategic-ally manipulating what can be detected of the "super-personal self-organizing forces which create spontaneous orders" in nature and society (Hayek 2012, 54). Markets are apprehended as ecosystems exposed to the evolutionary pressure of natural selection and competition; adaptation is regarded as the guiding principle of social formations; and resilience characterizes both natural capital and social systems (Walker & Cooper 2011; Watts 2015). In the green neoliberal planet, the *homo economicus* merges with the *homo biologicus*; economic and species survival are one and the same thing. Malleable green citizens are asked to save the planet and themselves from extinction by con-forming to corporate agendas and state-led energy regimes. They fulfill their

---

[9] On neoliberal environmentalism, see Bakker (2015); Castree (2008); Ciplet & Roberts (2017); Heynen (2007); Parr (2014); Pellizzoni (2011). Dario Gentili has shed light on the neoliberal naturalization of crises (Gentili 2021).

[10] See The White House (2023) and Directorate-General for Communication of the European Commission (DG COMM) (2022).

[11] Neoliberal ecologies began to take shape when Cold War environmentalism acquired its distinctive planetary scope and the Earth became "One Earth" (Ward & Dubos 1972), the theatre of a US-led global environmental order of markets and ecosystems (Höhler 2015; Masco 2014).

duties when they behave as decarbonized eco-consumers and defuse their eco-anxiety in the marketplace of net-zero corporate sustainability.

It is against this state of nature that multispecies ecologies envision a creative web of life. I agree with Rob Nixon: we should not be surprised that "millions of readers and viewers become magnetized by the hitherto arcane field of plant communication" (Nixon 2022).[12] Public science writing has popularized the multispecies understanding of communication, intelligence, and sentience because of "a widespread discontent with neoliberalism's antipathy to cooperative ways of being" (Nixon 2022). The contemporary appeal of vegetal altruism (Kohn 2013; Mancuso 2021) is a reaction to the political ascendency of Reaganism and Thatcherism, a rebuttal of the economistic interpretation of natural history. The counter-discourse of plant sociability exhibits the divergent trajectories of subjectivization fostered by the environmental crisis of presence. Their respective figures are the *homo economicus* and the symbiont, alternative modes of being subject, rooted either in competition or collaboration, ecocide or livability.

We can trace the codevelopment of these paradigms back to the infancy of neoliberal ideology. In the 1970s, while the "Chicago Boys" – the Chilean economists trained at the University of Chicago – fetishized individualism and experimented with policies of deregulation and privatization in Augusto Pinochet's military dictatorship (Mirowski & Plehwe 2009, 305–46), the atmospheric chemist James Lovelock elaborated the Gaia hypothesis with biologist Lynn Margulis (Lovelock & Margulis 1974). By altering the composition of rocks, water, and the atmosphere, life on Gaia has created the conditions for its own existence (Lovelock 1979). The Earth was initially conceived by Lovelock in purely cybernetic terms, as an organism–machine that regulates its internal feedback loops in order to preserve the fragile equilibrium of the biosphere.[13] Thanks to Margulis's contribution, the Gaia hypothesis has grown into a sweeping vision of symbiotic planetary life: "Gaia is just symbiosis as seen from space," the depiction of "fellow symbionts" that "abide in the same place at the same time, literally touching each other or even inside each other" (Margulis 1998, 2).

Margulis's advocacy of "symbiosis everywhere" (7) has galvanized multispecies thinking: with symbiosis, socioecological thought has put aside the Darwinian drama of individual organisms fighting for survival and hoarding a scarce pool of resources. If, also, the eukaryotic cell is a compound of bacteria,

---

[12] See Suzanne Simard's popularization of forest ecology (Jabr 2020).

[13] Gaia is the old Greek name for the Earth and its mythological personification. James Lovelock's cybernetic interpretation of planetary life has been questioned by critical theory (Clarke 2017). On Isabelle Stengers and the feminist reworking of the Gaia hypotesis, see Tola (2016).

then life is a "rhizomatic evolutionary schema" that functions through alliances and horizontal exchanges (Ansell-Pearson 1997, 134). In Gilles Deleuze and Felix Guattari's *A Thousand Plateaus*, symbioses sustain a flat ontology of collective becomings and dissolve stable selves and organisms (Deleuze & Guattari 1987, 242). Life spreads, resonates, and traverses bodies as a material, impersonal animation, a machine-like activity combining and recombining affects and movements. Taken up by Donna Haraway and more-than-human thought, multispecies thinking proliferates as "a new genre of writing and mode of research" (Kirksey & Helmreich 2010, 545), celebrating the creative flows of life.

In the wake of universal symbiosis, social animals, plants, and living things of all sorts have questioned the right of neoliberalism to set the standard of personhood and celebrate selfishness and competition as evolutionary principles (Donaldson & Kymlicka 2011; Tsing et al. 2017). Since biologically "we have never been individuals" (Gilbert, Sapp, & Tauber 2012), human exceptionalism can be overcome by thinking with "a host of companions in sympoietic threading, felting, tangling, tracking, and sorting" (Haraway 2016, 31). As Anna Tsing puts it, "human nature is an interspecies relationship" (Kirksey, Schuetze, & Helmreich 2014, 2). Life is animated by subtle relations that cross plants, animals, and humans; coevolution and multiple "involutions" of species dissolve biological boundaries and individualities (Hustak & Myers 2012). Life forces converge creatively in human and other-than-human bodies (Mussgnug 2019). Also communication, as revealed by ecosemiotics, is a pervasive relational activity that creates and sustains multispecies communities. Semiosis takes place "on different levels of the biological world ranging from cells to ecosystems, and both inside and between organisms" (Maran 2020, 1). Human exchanges and interpretations of signs participate in a biological tapestry of conversations: "living nature itself, the ecosystem, is predominantly semiotic by being based on sign regulation in its each and every joint" (Maran 2020, 59).

From multispecies approaches we have learned that biology and society are "relational through and through."[14] To exist "is already to be positioned in a certain environment and committed to the relationships this entails" (Ingold 2000, 149). We cannot "counterpose the land to its inhabitants along the axis of a dichotomy between the animate and the inanimate" (Ingold 2000, 149): nature and culture, geochemical and biological processes are different aspects of the continuum of life, an ecological plane of transformations, punctuated by hybrid selves of various degrees of mobility and animation, consciousness and

---

[14] See James Gibson's influential concept of "affordances" (Gibson 2015, 120–35).

sentience (Descola 2005; Viveiros de Castro 2014).[15] Ecologies from the Global South have drawn the political consequences of this refusal of human-centered personhood: relationality is "in the Earth itself, in the endless and ceaselessly changing weave of life on which all life depends" (Escobar 2018, xi). The goal of emancipative struggles is to draw the political implications of the relational matrix that encloses all living beings (12). As an alternative to the one world of neoliberal globalization, multispecies ecologies feed the decolonial utopia of the pluriverse. The term "pluriverse" began to circulate in Latin America's circles in the mid-1990s. Borrowed from William James's pluralist cosmology and inspired by the Zapatistas' vision of "a world where many worlds fit" (Ejército Zapatista de Liberación Nacional 1996), it soon grew into a paradigm of socioecological coexistence. The pluriverse describes a planet characterized by the mutual care of heterogeneous and interdependent life-forms (Kothari et al. 2019; Reiter 2018).[16]

But what does relationality mean, when we frame it from the perspective of geobodies that are not alive? What are the principles of a third ecology that does not interpret other-than-human forces as an expression of life? How can earth-beings be subjective as well as nonliving?

1.3 Persons and Subjects

Beyond life, relational ecologies have revealed the interconnectedness of natures across the human/nonhuman divide. They have mapped the processes that transform and aggregate "porous bodies" (Iovino 2014, 102), the impersonal becomings of an Earth "permeated by unformed, unstable matters, by flows in all directions, by free intensities or nomadic singularities, by mad or transitory particles" (Deleuze & Guattari 1987, 40). The third ecology thinks with social processes and nonliving beings, with geobodies caught at the intersection of divergent forces. For the Aymara and Quechua Indigenous communities in the Andes and their "culture of stones" (Dean 2010), sacred mountains are subjects with whom they engage ritually but they are also geological formations that are mined, deforested, and dammed by transnational

---

[15] Not all multispecies anthropologists share the view that life and nonlife consist of degrees of animation in a vital continuum. Eduardo Kohn attributes vitality only to semiotic organisms: "life thinks; stones don't . . . living beings are loci of selfhood," stones are not (Kohn 2013, 100).

[16] Feminist collectives in South America have transformed awareness of human and nonhuman reproductive struggles into a methodology of political resistance. The creative forces of reproduction of life are captured by the regime of accumulation of natural capital and regulated by transnational corporations (Barca 2020): crops are enslaved in monocultures, unpaid women's bodies are used as reproducers of labor (Federici 2004). Since "there is no ontological difference between territory and the body" and "what is done to the body is done to the territory and vice versa," then emancipation will have to come from the *cuerpo-territorio* of entangled women and natures subjected to the violence of extractive industries (Zaragocin & Caretta 2021, 1508).

corporations. Marisol de la Cadena's notion of earth-beings captures this hybrid composition of geobodies. In Andean stones and springs, "heterogeneous worlding practices" come together to construct ecopolitical subjects (de la Cadena & Blaser 2018, 6). In this Element, building on the notion of earth-beings, I draw the contour of a decolonial ecology that disentangles geobodies from the language of life and the *dispositif* of Western personhood. My hypothesis is that stones, valleys, air, ice, and waterbodies are revealed as ecopolitical subjects by the current crisis of presence. And their nonliving subjectivity cannot be contained anymore by anthropological constructions of animism and totemism that, from colonial times, have confined them in Indigenous lifeworlds.[17]

To approach earth-beings without reproducing the biocentric language of life, I assume that personhood and subjecthood should be carefully disentangled. In 1981, reflecting on paintings of marble blocks, the Italian writer Italo Calvino published a short text entitled "Being Stone" (Calvino 2005). Calvino's commentary illustrates an essential presupposition of the third ecology: geobodies are subjects without being persons. "I am a stone. I repeat: a stone" (419). The protagonist of this micro-essay is a stone-philosopher who narrates the world as seen by stones. Calvino confronts us with the paradox of a subject that eludes all human and biological connotations: "I am a stone among other stones in a world of stones, where there are only stones, blocks and chunks and splinters and megaliths and dolmens" (420). The fiction of a stone as a narrative subject allows Calvino to separate subjectivity from personhood. There are no analogies between the biological world of humans and the world of stones. The form, matter, time, and space of being a stone exclude man: "stones remain and the human passes . . . in this stone-world there is neither a before nor an after" (420). Also the "power of edification" of stones, exploited by humans to build their own artificial universe, "would be enacted even if men were not there" (420). The natural history of stones is wounded by man's tools, by the violence of quarrying, blasting, cutting. Stones and men meet, but without stones being able to act as a center of experience, consciousness, or purpose. To be a stone for Calvino means to be a subject, not a person.

In this Element, Calvino's distinction between personhood and subjecthood serves as a thread to extricate the subjectivity of nonliving earth-beings from the living selves of multispecies ethnographies, which hinge on the bioanthropological language of other-than-human personhood. Geobodies are unassimilable subjects: their inhuman scales and materiality do not participate in a universal

---

[17] Descola (2005) and Viveiros de Castro (2004). On unruly natural subjects, see the collaborative project "Unruly Natures" (https://unrulynatures.ch./).

biomorphic vitality. Elizabeth Povinelli has stubbornly asked a decisive question: "What happens when we create solidarity between humans and more-than-humans through the idea of the human person?" (Povinelli 2021, 124). We can rightly be suspicious of the expansive tendencies of Western personifications and handle with prudence the language of personhood. As Roberto Esposito argues, the separation of persons and things emerged at the confluence between Greek philosophy, Roman law, and Christianity: "Since Roman times, this distinction has been reproduced in all modern codifications, becoming the presupposition that serves as the implicit ground for all other types of thought – for legal but also philosophical, economic, political, and ethical reasoning" (Esposito 2015, 2–3). Western personhood is grounded in this tradition, which has severed the *persona* from the *res* (thing) with the goal of conflating humanity and ownership, personhood and mastery over slaves and their bodies. Appropriation of something – that thus becomes a *res* – by someone who claims to be a subject – a *persona* – is the foundation of modern Western political thought.

Within this logic of domination, the soul hegemonizes the body and its biological fabric. Only through an act of self-subjection does the person achieve a formal unity.[18] In reality, the *persona* is split and held together by a hierarchical apparatus: the soul presides over the body, the *logos* over the *bios*, as the master over the slave, thus reproducing the original separation between the theatrical mask (the original Greek meaning of *persona*) and the face of the actor who wore it:

> It has been well established that the Greek etymology of the term [*persona*] refers to the theatrical mask placed on the actor's face, but precisely for this reason the *persona* was never identical to the face. The word later referred to the type of character depicted in the play, but this, too, was never the same as the actor who interpreted it from one occasion to the next. The law seems to have reproduced this element of duality or duplicity at the heart of humanity. *Persona* was not the individual as such, but only its legal status, which varied on the basis of its power relationships with others. (30)

At the core of Western personhood lies a process of division and domination, modeled on the primacy of the human as possessor – of a mask, of social and political roles, of properties, and other humans.[19] When we speak the language of the person, we presuppose the split and the hierarchization of humans and nonhumans that the oxymoron of "other-than-human personhood" is striving to overcome.

---

[18] See also Michel Foucault: "The subject is either divided inside himself or divided from others. This process objectivizes him" (Dreyfus & Rabinow 2014, 208).

[19] On the transition from trust to domination and the corresponding transformation of personhood, which took place when hunters and gatherers shifted from predation to pastoralism and domestication, see Ingold (2000, 61–76).

In the Americas, the legal apparatus of the proprietorial *persona* has stripped slaves and Indigenous societies of their lands and humanity, and transformed an entire continent into a *terra nullius* ("nobody's land"), an object for mineral and agricultural extraction. Esposito's conceptual history of the Western *persona* thus converges with the analytics of New World slavery laid out by Franz Fanon, Édouard Glissant, Saidiya Hartman, Sylvia Wynter, and black/decolonial studies. In their account, the order of knowledge to which personhood belongs is "enabled by proprietorial notions of the self: humanity and individuality acted to tether, bind, and oppress" in the plantations' forced assemblages of black bodies, crops, and animals (Hartman 1997, 5–6). Liberal personhood obscures the political foundation of the coloniality of power; legal personifications and psychological depersonalizations mirror the historical ferocity of possession and dispossession of humans and territories: "Western and Westernized global selves" were produced by the coloniality of being as "biocentric (and neo-Darwinianly chartered) subjects" (Wynter 2015, 67). Before multispecies ecologies weaved together hybrid organisms and earthly forces, the "entanglements of bondage and liberty" shaped "the liberal imagination of freedom, fuelled the emergence and expansion of capitalism, and spawned proprietorial conceptions of the self" (Hartman 1997, 115). A constitutive relationship binds individual freedom with slavery, requiring that we map the "articulations of freedom and the forms of subjection they beget" (116).[20]

The liberal archetype of this nexus is exemplified by John Locke's theory of property and personhood. A beneficiary of the slave trade and the founding father of liberalism, Locke coauthored *The Fundamental Constitutions for the Government of Carolina* (1669) as secretary to the Earl of Shaftesbury, one of the Lords Proprietors of Carolina, and he actively justified the link between individual personhood and private ownership:

> Because land cultivated in common cannot be considered appropriated or of any value until it is enclosed by the individual, Amerindians engaged in agricultural activities as a collective unit, rather than as individuals within enclosed ground, will have no exclusive right to their property ... Title to property – that is, the right to exclude others from it – can only be claimed, by definition, by the individual. (Arneil 1996, 141)

Personhood as a center of experience – be it moral, legal, or psychological – is for Locke inseparable from the juridico-political connotations of being an individual possessor who alienates other humans and nonhumans from this essential "freedom."

---

[20] See also Yusoff (2018).

In the next sections, I will outline the features of a decolonial political ecology in which geobodies deactivate the tenets of Western liberal personhood. Released by our "global interhuman and environmental situation" (Wynter 1996, 8), a profound crisis of presence is producing subjects that do not comply with anthropocentric worldviews. Mountains in the Andes (Section 2), erratics and a landfill in the Swiss Alps (Sections 3 and 4), and the "sacred stones" of the Standing Rock Sioux Reservation (Section 5) will allow me to reflect on the juridical personification of ecosystems carried out by the rights of nature movement and detect the persistent attempts by biological and cultural person-hood to contain the unruly subjectivity of geobodies.[21]

As I conclude this Introduction, the planetary crisis of presence brings me back to a preoccupation expressed by the nineteenth-century poet Giacomo Leopardi: How can we oppose the "great alliance of intelligent beings against nature and everything that lacks intelligence?" (Leopardi 1997, 890 [4280]).[22] Being a stone, as in Calvino's text, disproves the juridical civilization founded on the Roman law according to which the proprietorial human person is "the absolute master of the animal that dwells inside" (Esposito 2015, 31) and of all the surrounding beings. Stones, air, and waterbodies do not communicate, feel, and think as biological organisms; and yet, we share with them the "terrestrial condition" (Gosselin & gé Bartoli 2022). Isn't it time to also perceive and engage Western earth-beings as ecopolitical subjects?

2 Earth-Beings

Marisol de la Cadena and Mario Blaser ask that we recognize the epistemic configurations determining what is a subject and what is an object, who can speak and who cannot. Their definition of that exercise in ethnographic thinking from the Global South is political ontology, a cross-examination of the meaning of personhood in a discursive field designed by Western categories.[23] Political ontology involves "things like mountains and forests that emerge as resources through some practices but also as persons through other practices" (de la Cadena & Blaser 2018, 5), paradoxical entities that question the universality of systems ecologies.[24]

---

[21] The role attributed to the subjectivity of geobodies distinguishes the third ecology from the methodologies of political geology (Bobbette & Donovan 2019; Clark & Yusoff, 2017).

[22] On Giacomo Leopardi's political ecology, see Luisetti (2021).

[23] "Political ontology wants to enable political thought and practice beyond the onto-epistemic limits of modern politics and what its practice allows" (de la Cadena & Blaser 2018, 6).

[24] On Isabelle Stengers's influence on decolonial political ontology, see de la Cadena (2023). The Environmental Justice Atlas documents several ontological conflicts between geobodies and natural resources. See, for instance, the Woodside's Burrup Gas Hub in Western Australia (https://ejatlas.org/conflict/scarborough-gas-project), the Snowbowl project in the San

In the dramatic context of South America's conflicts between neoliberal policies and Indigenous movements, disagreement on the different "ways of distributing and establishing what exists, and their mutual relations" (Blaser 2013, 23) has lost any scholarly pedantry. During the early 2000s, the "Water War" in the Bolivian city of Cochabamba, a struggle that inspired anti-neoliberal environmentalism in the following decade, the alliance between Indigenous and non-Indigenous protesters successfully "opposed the privatization of the public water system ... that the World Bank has negotiated in exchange of USD 600 million in debt relief" (Tola 2018, 30).[25] For the activists in Cochabamba, asking if the water is the "blood of the Pachamama" or an ecosystem service regulated by financial capital was not a scholarly preoccupation (30). Water exceeds the language of neoliberal ecological infrastructures: it is an aspect of Pachamama, the Andean deity embodying the Earth's generative powers, with whom Bolivian communities have forged communal bonds of reciprocity since precolonial times. Indigenous peasant organizations (*ayllus*) mobilized to "defend what they considered as an ancestral right to engage with hydric resources."[26]

In this section, I will introduce the reader to the personifications of nature that accompanied Latin America's early 2000s leftist tide. The Ecuadorian and Bolivian constitutionalization of Pachamama and the international movement of the rights of nature are the direct outcome of this political process (Landivar & Ramillien 2017). I will then address other prominent cases of ecopolitical personification, which have sparked the hopes of activists around the world. Andean peasant struggles against neoliberalism have amplified the planetary subjectivization of nature that I described in Section 1. The Indigenous communities that resist land-grabbing and pollution do not share the same degree of vulnerability with activists occupying airports and water basins in Europe.[27] But mountains, rivers, and valleys in the Global South and the Global North have now joined plants and animals in a planetary insurgence.[28]

Francisco Peaks, United States (https://bit.ly/3PSevpC), and Brazil's mega-dam, Teles Pires, in the Tapajós basin (https://bit.ly/3PnU8iQ).

[25] "In the mid-1980s, Bolivia became a kind of living laboratory for Harvard economist Jeffrey Sachs to test the ideas of structural adjustment and neoliberal trade rules. These reached fruition in the mid-1990s, as privatization of state sectors, large-scale enclosures, massive reductions of state employment, deregulation, decentralization, and free trade policies were implemented through a sharp recession, increasing inequality, and contraction of state services" (Hecht 2013, xxi).

[26] Uhel (2019), my translation.

[27] See the ZAD of Notre-Dame-de-Lande website (https://zad.nadir.org/), Gosselin & gé Bartoli (2022, 73–106), and Lindgaard (2018).

[28] On animal rights, see Donaldson & Kymlicka (2011).

2.1 Mother Earth

The Indigenous figure of Pachamama is the protagonist of the Universal Declaration of Rights of Mother Earth issued in Cochabamba at the 2010 World People's Conference on Climate Change and the Rights of Mother Earth (Rights of Mother Earth 2010). This historic event – sponsored by Evo Morales, a trade union leader of coca growers who, in 2005, became the first Indigenous president of a South American state – made Mother Earth (*Madre Tierra* in Spanish, a translation of Pachamama) a political subject of global relevance. The choice of the city of Cochabamba signaled a continuity with the Water War of the early 2000s and placed Bolivia at the forefront of the resistance movement against neoliberalism. An international network of 35,000 activists and NGOs from 140 countries joined the alliance of Bolivian Indigenous organizations and demanded climate and environmental justice for Mother Earth/Pachamama.

The Universal Declaration of Rights of Mother Earth was part of the constituent process that transformed Bolivia into a plurinational state, formally recognizing the political autonomy of its thirty-six Indigenous nations. Drafted by a coalition of Bolivia's largest peasant and Indigenous organizations, the Declaration envisioned Pachamama as a self-regulating organism, animated by a vitality that runs through its planetary body:

(1) Mother Earth is a living being.

(2) Mother Earth is a unique, indivisible, self-regulating community of interrelated beings that sustains, contains and reproduces all beings.

(3) Each being is defined by its relationships as an integral part of Mother Earth . . . .

(4) The inherent rights of Mother Earth are inalienable in that they arise from the same source as existence.

(5) Mother Earth and all beings are entitled to all the inherent rights recognized in this Declaration without distinction of any kind, such as may be made between organic and inorganic beings, species, origin, use to human beings, or any other status.

(6) Just as human beings have human rights, all other beings also have rights which are specific to their species or kind and appropriate for their role and function within the communities within which they exist.

(7) The rights of each being are limited by the rights of other beings and any conflict between their rights must be resolved in a way that maintains the integrity, balance and health of Mother Earth.

(Rights of Mother Earth 2010)

This manifesto of ecocentrism personified Pachamama as a nonhuman subject of rights, a major achievement of Bolivia's Indigenous uprising. At the same time, as advocated in its Preamble, the Declaration has served Evo Morales's diplomatic agenda and reinforced his moral leadership against the Washington Consensus:

> We, the peoples and nations of Earth: considering that we are all part of Mother Earth, an indivisible, living community of interrelated and inter-dependent beings with a common destiny; gratefully acknowledging that Mother Earth is the source of life, nourishment and learning and provides everything we need to live well; recognizing that the capitalist system and all forms of depredation, exploitation, abuse and contamination have caused great destruction, degradation and disruption of Mother Earth, putting life as we know it today at risk through phenomena such as climate change … proclaim this Universal Declaration of the Rights of Mother Earth, and call on the General Assembly of the United Nation to adopt it, as a common standard of achievement for all peoples and all nations of the world. (Rights of Mother Earth 2010)

Propelled by this internationalist eco-Pachamanismo, after Cochabamba the subjectivity of earth-beings has inspired alternatives to the neoliberal global-ization of nature.[29] Andean earth-beings have merged with the well-being of ecosystems and nurtured a growing movement of Earth jurisprudence and planetary sustainability (La Follette & Maser 2019).

Unfortunately, the state laws personifying Pachamama as Mother Earth are the outcome of a deceptive political agenda and disempowering epistemic equivocation.[30] While the leftist populist governments of Evo Morales in Bolivia and Rafael Correa in Ecuador were promoting an ecological variety of Pachamama that appealed also to Western environmentalism, at home these governments pursued a "transition to socialism" entrenched in extractivism and resource nationalism (Riofrancos 2020). The formal recognition of Indigenous values went hand in hand with a modernist policy of development that relied heavily on the extraction of natural resources: "In Bolivia, the extractive wave includes mining, hydrocarbon exploitation, the advancement of agribusiness, and more recently a series of energy projects" (Svampa 2019, 34). Justified by Morales and Correa as a necessary phase of development,[31] these policies turned out to resemble colonial methods of predatory extracti-vism: "social and environmental impacts linked to the large scale of the undertakings; high level of conflict linked to them; limited economic benefits,

---

[29] Pachamama's ecology also had a palpable influence on Pope Francis's Encyclical Letter *Laudato sii*: "The laws found in the Bible dwell on relationships, not only among individuals but also with other living beings" (Pope Francis 2015, 50).

[30] On equivocation in the Andean–Amazonian context, see Viveiros de Castro (2004).

[31] On resource nationalism as a transition to socialism, see the work of Morales's collaborator and Vice-President of Bolivia, Álvaro García Linera (García Linera 2012).

(re)privatization of the economy, territorial fragmentation, and distorts of the productive apparatus" (50). Correa's government responded to Indigenous resistance to extraction projects with "the criminalization and judicialization of environmental protest. Criminal trials sentenced spokespeople for indigenous organizations to up to ten years imprisonment" (35).[32]

Mother Earth's impotence as a jurisprudential subject to stand up against the predation of resources rests on the legal formulation of the Bolivian constitution, which lacks binding mechanisms of implementation of the rights of nature and, under the banner of "redistributive justice," emphasizes the development of hydrocarbons, mining, and metallurgy (Calzadilla & Kotzé 2018, 418). But an even greater menace endangers Pachamama: its metamorphosis into an ecosystemic female subject, Mother Earth, prolongs the assimilation of earth-beings initiated by Catholic missionaries and European conquistadores. As in colonial times, an ambiguous politics of recognition incorporates Andean geobodies into Christian symbols of female fertility, subjecting Pachamama to the dualistic cosmology of male sovereignty/female reproductivity (Lugones 2010). The celebration of Mother Earth's reproductive powers recalls popular colonial representations such as the Virgin Mary of Potosí, the silver-rich mountain at the heart of the Spanish Empire (Tola 2018, 28). Bolivian feminist collectives have denounced the "'colonial gender system' that turns the vitality of the earth into a motherly figure ... locking up this earth-being, and with it Bolivian women, into a subordinated identity" (35–6). Against this gendered personification of Pachamama, they have affirmed the incommensurability of Indigenous natures. Pachamama is not a benevolent Mother Earth: "radical differences between nature and Pachamama cannot be undone" (de la Cadena 2015, 284).

2.2 Wild Law

Beyond the Andes, encounters between threatened ecosystems and the state are spreading a corpus of Earth jurisprudence, a "wild law" that extends legal personhood to subjectivized natures: rivers, glaciers, valleys, urban air (Maloney & Burdon 2014). The legal consolidation of other-than-human persons can empower Indigenous claims but it also infects natural subjects with the virus of personhood. Since Aristotle, in the Western political tradition, humans are political subjects because they alone possess the *logos*, the power of speech.

---

[32] "Over the past 30 years the extractive industries in Bolivia, having been developed in protected natural areas and indigenous territories, have contributed to the degradation of one third of the national territory" (Calzadilla & Kotzé 2018, 404).

Man is a political animal as a speaking subject.[33] In view of this premise, Christopher D. Stone, a pioneer of the rights of nature, has acknowledged the bias of legal personhood. Since nature cannot speak the language of humans, natural beings must be treated by the law of humans as legal incompetents:

> It is no answer to say that streams and forests cannot have standing because streams and forests cannot speak. Corporations cannot speak, either; nor can states, estates, infants, incompetents, municipalities, or universities. Lawyers speak for them, as they customarily do for the ordinary citizen with legal problems. One ought, I think, to handle the legal problems of natural objects as one does the problems of legal incompetents – human beings who have become vegetative . . . The guardian (or "conservator" or "committee" – the terminology varies) then represents the incompetent in his legal affairs. (Stone 2010, 8)[34]

This earnest assessment of the logic of Western legal personhood reveals the foundations of Bruno Latour's politics of nature, the most influential ecophilosophy of our times. His advocacy of things and their parliaments rests on Aristotle's logocentric presupposition, the *bios politikós* ("political life"). For Latour, nonhumans "are implicated in a great number of *speech impediments*" (Latour 1999, 63), they cannot speak on their own and therefore are in need of spokespersons: experts, science studies scholars, European philosophers. As speech incompetents, natures and things cannot participate in Western democracy without the assistance of mediators and guardians. Latour's unrepentant logocentrism helps clarify the link between personhood and exclusion: "I do not claim that things speak 'on their own' . . . I have not required human subjects to share the right of speech of which they are so justly proud with galaxies, neurons, cells, viruses, plants, and glaciers" (68). Natural entities are "mute things" that come to visibility thanks to the "speaking subject of the political tradition" (68). Within this logocentric logic, it is impossible to attribute political subjectivity to plants and glaciers. Because personhood is the outcome of multiple exclusions, the right of speech that Latour is not willing to share with natural subjects is conferred by a proprietorial person at the expense of other beings, which are evicted not only from their lifeworld but also from their subjectivity.

Western personhood also casts its long shadow in the most successful recent legal personification of a natural being. In March 2017, after 140 years of disputes and negotiations, New Zealand's national parliament passed the Te Awa Tupua Act which granted to the Whanganui River – considered an ancestor by the

---

[33] "The supremely political destiny of man is attested by a sign: the possession of the logos, that is, of speech, which expresses" (Rancière 1999, 2).

[34] Christopher Stone's (1972) text initiated the legal debate on rights of nature in common law.

Māori – the same duties, rights, powers, and liabilities as a legal person, "from the mountains to the sea, incorporating all its physical and metaphysical elements."[35] Since then, the relationship of the Māori with the river is enshrined in law, respecting an essential Māori principle: "Ko au te Awa, ko te Awa ko au" ("I am the river and the river is me") (O'Donnell 2018, 164). However, if we read between the lines, New Zealand's groundbreaking legislation hides a poisonous gift. The river owns itself through an artificial entity, the legal form of the Whanganui River, which is protected by two guardians, one appointed by the national government and the other by the Māori. While symbolically recognizing the Māori's nonanthropocentric political ontology, the legal arrangement denies them any direct sovereignty over the riverbed (Salmond 2014). The river co-owns its body with the Crown, whereas the Māori own neither the river nor its water and catchment: "The legislation creating legal rights for the Whanganui River expressly states that nothing in the Act 'creates, limits, transfers, extinguishes, or otherwise affects any rights to, or interests in, water'. This means that the river, although it includes the entire catchment from the mountains to the sea, does not own the rights to its own water" (O'Donnell 2018, 165). What kind of earth-being, what diminished subject, is a river that cannot care for its own water?

Shortly after the approval of that historic bill by the parliament of New Zealand, the Supreme Court of Uttarakhand also ruled, in July 2017, that the Indian Ganga and Yamuna Rivers were living entities with the status of legal persons. Personified European rivers and glaciers followed suit, emulating the legal achievements of the Indigenous politics of nature. In September 2020, a popular assembly concerned with the well-being of the Rhône River – which crosses Switzerland and France, flowing for 813 kilometers through Lausanne, Geneva and Lyon, from a melting glacier in the Alps to the delta in the Mediterranean Sea near Marseille – launched the "Call of the Rhône," a mobilization to recognize the juridical personhood of the river.[36] The goal was to promote actions at the scale of the ecosystem of the Rhône, affirming its rights to "dignity, security, preservation, and integrity" across national legal and political systems, territorial boundaries, and special interests.[37]

---

[35] Whanganui District Council, Te Awa Tupua – Whanganui River Settlement (www.whanga nui.govt.nz/About-Whanganui/Our-District/Te-Awa-Tupua-Whanganui-River-Settlement) and Bourgeois-Gironde 2020. The Te Awa Tupua Act superseded the 2014 Whanganui River Deed of Settlement between the New Zealand Government and the Whanganui Iwi (a Māori tribe), which recognized the legal personhood of the river. Referencing this model, in November 2016 the Constitutional Court of Colombia recognized the Río Atrato, its tributaries, and the basin as a juridical subject.

[36] Assemblée populaire du Rhône (www.assembleepopulairedurhone.org).

[37] Since 2019, another informal "parliament of the river," the parliament of the Loire, has united ecologists, artists, intellectuals, residents, and activists campaigning for the rights of nature of

The iconic French glacier of the Mer de Glace, on the Mont Blanc massif, has also been addressed as a legal subject at the hearings of the International Rights of Nature Tribunal.[38] "Humans are causing the Mer de Glace to disappear. It is urgent to recognize its right to existence. The Mer de Glace's right to regenerate and upholding of its natural cycles must also be acknowledged."[39] The Tribunal demands that the "interdependence between humans and non-humans" acquires the force of law. The glacier is a subject linked to humans through the planetary body of Mother Earth, so rights traditionally attributed to humans and corporations must be extended to threatened natural beings. In Europe, the most significant recent case is that of the Mar Menor in the Murcia region of Spain. In September 2022, following a popular legislative initiative, the Spanish Senate passed a law granting legal personality to this coastal lagoon and its basin. It is the first European legal text to recognize an ecosystem as a subject of law. These earth-beings are joining the ecosystems that administrations in the United States have recognized through ordinances as bearing enforceable legal rights of nature: from clean water and air in Pittsburgh, Pennsylvania (2010) to Lake Erie in Ohio (2019).[40] In the "Great Planetary Inside" of the Anthropocene (Iovino 2019), earth-beings are subjectivized as legal persons to battle states and corporations in court and affirm the rights of other-than-humans. But the incorporation of earth-beings into wild law compels geobodies to speak the language of litigation, confining them in the labyrinth of Western biocentric and logocentric personhood.

2.3 Life

Legal scholars remind us that "in any jurisdiction influenced, however indirectly, by Roman jurisprudence," the enduring fiction of the legal person perseveres as the "dispositif that binds biological and symbolic registers into a single juridical-anthropological institution" (Mussawir & Parsley 2017, 45). Western legal systems are erected on Roman law's proprietorial foundation, an artifice that presupposes only the "unity of a patrimony" (Thomas 1998, 100). On this ground, Christianity has performed a metaphysical unification of personhood and sublimated the technicality of Roman law into the sacred unity of the moral

---

the river, through art–science projects, debates, studies, assemblies, and public hearings (Manifeste de Loire, www.parlementdeloire.org/).

[38] The International Rights of Nature Tribunal (www.rightsofnaturetribunal.org/) is an offshoot of the Global Alliance for the Rights of Nature, a global network of organizations promoting the rights of nature (www.garn.org/). The Tribunal issues symbolic resolutions and "aims to create a forum for people from all around the world to speak on behalf of nature, to protest the destruction of the Earth."

[39] International Rights of Nature Tribunal (www.rightsofnaturetribunal.org/cases/glacier-case/).

[40] United Nations, Harmony with Nature (www.harmonywithnatureun.org/).

person, an indissoluble compound of body and spirit.[41] Natural entities are now joining this field of biosocial morality.

A lawsuit in Northern Australia brought by the Aboriginal Areas Protection Authority against the Singapore-based mining company OM Manganese Ltd. (Aboriginal Areas Protection Authority 2013) illustrates the pervasiveness of biocentric personhood. The prosecution benefited from legislation that has protected Aboriginal geobodies in Australia since the late 1970s, decades before the rights of nature movement spread worldwide from the Andes. In the Darwin Magistrates' Court, OM Manganese Ltd. was fined USD 150,000 – a mostly symbolic amount – for damaging and desecrating Two Women Sitting Down, a geological formation which is also an Aboriginal sacred site: "This site has great significance to the custodians and relates to a Dreaming story about a marsupial rat and a bandicoot who had a fight over bush tucker. As the creation ancestors fought, their blood spilled out, turning the rock a dark-red colour that is now associated with manganese" (Aboriginal Areas Protection Authority 2013). OM Manganese Ltd. continued to blast and excavate ore next to Two Women Sitting Down, "despite knowing that a collapse was imminent. Ultimately, the site collapse totaled 17,000 cubic metres of ore, soil and vegetation" (Aboriginal Areas Protection Authority 2013).

Reflecting on this case, Elizabeth Povinelli has discussed the biocentric bias of the law of persons (Povinelli 2016, 30–56; 2021, 121–6). Indigenous activists are conscious that legal personifications of sacred sites and ecosystems are a provisional tactic to slow and deflect the "juridical innovations of capitalism" (Povinelli 2021, 121). However, the activists' attempts are curtailed by the logic of biological personhood, defeated by the "epidermal enclosures" of the living:

> The Aboriginal Areas Protection Authority must define the borders and boundaries of every site that Indigenous owners and custodians seek to register. . . . A site can have its personal space, but this space must conform to what a living agent, or person, is within Western law and imaginaries. . . . This ancestral presence must appear in the shape of Western living things. (125)

The mineral body of Two Women Sitting Down has condemned it to destruction: OM Manganese Ltd. has been allowed to excavate around the site, disregarding its nonliving region of existence. Despite the legal activists' attempts to turn Two Women Sitting Down's personhood against corporations, other-than-human earth-beings are crushed by the imaginary of life. Settler law

---

[41] Also "corporations, religious foundations, etc., which have become 'persons'" are "what we still call by the term 'moral persons' ('legal entities')" (Mauss 1985, 19).

demands that Indigenous authorities shape person-like objects to grant them the right of political existence, an operation that legitimates their annihilation.[42]

Inanimate beings are admitted to a natural life that drags them along thresholds of dehumanization: Pachamama is confined to a gendered female body, Two Women Sitting Down is perceived as a minor organism. The continuum of vitality feeds gendered and racialized beings, subjectivities created "through a process of subjection or objectivization" (Esposito 2012b, 21).[43] On the contrary, as Povinelli notes, in Indigenous Australia "persons aren't persons: To say 'I am water' or 'We are water' does not make water a person. It makes water and me necessary for each other's existence without knowing exactly how or where we intersect" (Povinelli 2021, 125–6).

2.4 Tirakuna

We return to the Andean Indigenous formations that have inspired the constitutions of Bolivia and Ecuador. These sacred mountains, rocks, and rivers were subjects before rights of nature began to incorporate them in the prison of legal personhood. For centuries, the numinous beings of Andean societies have been considered by European chroniclers as threatening persons and pagan fetishes. Spanish extirpators of idols used the traditional Quechua term *wakas* (or *huacas*, *guacas*) to identify these puzzling "sacred" beings, mostly but not exclusively lithic, that could be natural, man-made or a combination of the two, spatially fixed or distributed, and which "could not readily be identified by appearance, material composition, or location" (Dean 2010, 2) (see Figure 1).

Wakas are topographic features such as mountaintops, hills, lakes, caves, stones, and springs, but also statues, representations of men and animals, and extraordinary beings such as twins, gigantic trees, and oddly shaped vegetables (Bray 2015, 7). Roman Catholic Spaniards struggled to grasp the meaning and appearance of these "idols" that could serve as shrines and altars and receive offerings; that in most instances were not anthropomorphic or zoomorphic, and yet were endowed with a peculiar personhood and sociality:

> *Wakas* often shared kin relations with members of the communities with whom they were associated. There are various reports, for example, of young women being wed to local *wakas* made of stone . . . . Elsewhere *wakas* were said to have sons and daughters who were typically identified as the mummified remains of revered community ancestors . . . *Wakas* were also able to speak, hear, and communicate – both among themselves and with human persons. (9)

---

[42] On personhood and rights as a "dispositif of power," see Vatter & De Leeuw (2019).

[43] "These two sets of relationships that connect bodies in the world are still understood as completely distinct, as if our bodies were cut in two, as if we had two bodies: a social, racialized, gendered, and sexualized body and an ecological, biologized, and medicalized body" (Ferdinand 2022, 205).

Figure 1 The Inca Capac Yupanqui consulting with the waka Pachayachachic (Murúa, 2004 [1590] cited in Bray 2015, 6).

Sharing a "continuum of animacy along with plants, animals, and human beings" (Dean 2010, 8) and belonging to a common sociopolitical space of reciprocity, ritual practices, and metamorphoses constituted the key features of pre-Hispanic *wakas*. Assimilated by the Incas into a complex system of religious state ideology and then subjected to centuries of Christian inculturation (Scott 2011), Andean *wakas* are still approached by Indigenous societies as generative but also bewildering beings. In the rituals, narratives, and political struggles of Andean *runakuna* (the people) (Ari 2014), *wakas* animate and also frighten and preannounce, protect and punish, deceive and heal, sharing emotions, feelings, and expressions with humans. *Wakas* persist as eccentric subjectivities and odd earthscapes, incommensurable with rights of nature and Mother Earth ecologies.

Anthropologists, sociologists, philosophers, historians of religions, archaeologists, and linguists have abandoned the Christian prejudices of early colonial chroniclers of Indigenous "superstitious" beliefs, and yet they are still baffled by the personhood of *wakas*. Is it a vestige of ancestral Andean animism? Or do *wakas* exist only within "broader lexical and grammatical fields" proper to Quechua speakers, so that their subjectivity cannot be universalized? (Mannheim & Salas Carreño 2015, 64). Marisol de la Cadena joins the debate on the nature of *wakas* with her ethnography of earth-beings, her translation of *tirakuna*, a commonly used Quechua term in current-day Peru.[44] But *tirakuna* are also known as "places," since they indicate "snowcapped peaks, barren hills, lakes, ridges, rock outcrops, springs, boulders," the "*apus* (literally, 'lords')" that "are not spirits who dwell in places, but the places themselves" (Allen 2016b, 425). De la Cadena's book is the fruit of her friendship and decade-long colaboring with Peruvian peasants, healers, and shamans Mariano and Nazario Turpo. Through extended conversations with the Turpos, de la Cadena discloses the close-knit practices that relate earth-beings with traditional medicine and mass tourism, ritual offerings, and political opposition to state violence and landlords' abuses.

Ausangate – the great Peruvian mountain-spirit that "local people remembered acting 'like a lawyer,' or 'like the president'" (de la Cadena 2015, 96) – and other *tirakuna* of the Andean Cordillera are the other-than-human protagonists of de la Cadena's ethnography. Mariano Turpo, "as a male born in the property of the hacienda Lauramarca, . . . inherited from his father the obligation to work as a *colono*, a form of servitude organized around the large landowners" (41). His confrontation with Lauramarca and the colonial system of land ownership made him a protagonist of the Peruvian land reform movement, which in the 1960s defeated debt peonage, a colonial form of enslavement. De la Cadena documents how Mariano's political activity unfolded in conjunction with the local geobody of Ausangate, with whom he regularly consulted using coca leaves: "If I know how to cure animals, it is because Ausangate wants me to know" (48) "Ausangate fought for us, in place of us . . . so that we would be free. That is why we are free, that is why all of Peru is free. . . . Ausangate is more than our father, more than our mother, more than anyone" (114). Listening to Mariano Turpo's words, de la Cadena realizes that Ausangate is a pluriversal earth-being, not a person-like deity: a spirit revealing how to relate to state authorities, a presence in a ceremony, a natural feature, a tricky ally, a political authority, a tourist destination (96–8).

De la Cadena's familiarity with the Turpos leads to a seminal intuition: *tirakuna* and *runakuna*, natural and human beings, coconstitute themselves as subjects beyond the threshold of nature and culture. They emerge simultaneously, linked by forms of attention and submission: Mariano and Nazario Turpo must first be able to "identify the request an earth-being makes or imposes to establish a relationship with it, then willfully [enter] into that relationship and always steadfastly [nurture] it. The relationship usually materializes in the form of a successful apprenticeship and eventual deployment of

---

[44] *Tirakuna* is a composite noun "made of *tierra*, the Spanish word for 'earth,' and pluralized with the Quechua suffix *kuna*" (de la Cadena 2015, xxiii).

practices that can be broadly understood as healing (or damaging)" (18). This process makes the *ayllu*, the traditional agrarian community, the place-based kin group of humans and nonhumans: "Through in-*ayllu* practices, *runakuna* and *tirakuna take-place*" (133). Peruvian earth-beings and people are in-*ayllu* when they forge obligations, devising practices of codetermination through offerings, commensality, divination, and healing. The beliefs in animated nature, the "worship of the hills" attributed to the Quechua and Aymara, are colonial translations of a socioecological relation with earth-beings rooted in the continuum of humans and nonhumans (22).

This interpretation of the *ayllu* by de la Cadena reformulates Jacques Rancière's theory of political subjectivity as a scandal in the distribution of entities within the constituted order (Rancière 1999). For Rancière, "politics is a matter of subjects": workers, women, the people that reconfigure the field of experience by saying and making visible what was not recognizable in the previous arrangement of the sensible (35). These subjects did not exist until they provoked an alternative "distribution of bodies, times, and spaces" (106). To come to the fore, they had to transform the "identities defined in the natural order of the allocation of functions and places (36). Any subjectivization is thus a "disidentification," which removes entities from the naturalness of a (36). In Rancière's model, political subjectivation is set in motion by the exposure of a wrong. An example is provided by the subjectivization of workers as proletarians: while workers were only a social function, bodies involved in an occupation, they could not disturb the constituted allocation of identities and present themselves on the political stage as subjects. Only when they addressed the wrong that confined them to this order of society, and affirmed their autonomous subjectivity as proletarians, could they became protagonists of another history, they became a "polemical universal" (39).

De la Cadena argues that mountains, stones, and lakes act as earth-beings when they expound the foundational wrong of Western politics: the exclusion of Indigenous and other-than-human beings from the fabric of social life. In Mariano Turpo's communication with Ausangate, the paradox of addressing rocks as petrified spirits challenges Peruvian secular politics and endows *tirakuna* with a distinct political subjectivity. Earth-beings object to the separation of nature and humanity designed by the colonial state and the Western classification of natures. They denounce the construction of a regime of visibility that keeps them sealed in the inanimate world. In the Andes, earth-beings with *runakuna* disrupt the "ontological division between nature and humanity, which also parts the ahistorical from the historical and grants power to the latter to certify the real" (de la Cadena 2015, 279). De la Cadena's reformulation of Rancière's theory of political subjectivity deactivates the biocentric language of Western personhood. We do not need to attribute to stones and water the vitality that we recognize in biological organisms.

Tirakuna's animation comes from other sources: it originates in the affective, ritual, and semiotic encounters with *runakuna*.

The Turpos' *mise-en-scène* of shamanic rituals deconstructs the managerial description of the environment as a purely natural domain and recomposes socionatural reality from the perspective of nonhuman entities.[45] Earth-beings and their Indigenous allies act as Rancière's women and proletarians: they are the "part of those who have no part" (Rancière 1999, 78). Whereas Rancière confines the disagreement about what counts as a political subject to human societies, de la Cadena extends it to assemblages of humans and nonhumans. Earth-beings are allowed to reset the political scene and present "modern politics with that which is impossible under its conditions" (de la Cadena 2015, 279) through consulting with mountain spirits with the help of coca leaves and asking that Ausangate nominates community leaders.[46] Andean earth-beings prove Rancière's key premise: "politics is not made up of power relationships; it is made up of relationships between worlds" (Rancière 1999, 42).

2.5 Storied Subjects

From the ethnographies of Andean earth-beings, we learn that *tirakuna* behave as subjects only in conjunction with *runakuna*, when they are engaged ritually and semiotically through acts of "reciprocal appropriation among beings of different ontological status" (Allen 2016a, 332). *Tirakuna* populate a "middle place," the "material 'mesh' of meanings, properties, and processes, in which human and nonhuman players are interlocked in networks that produce undeniable signifying forces" (Iovino & Oppermann 2014, 1–2).[47] Mountains and rivers, stones and artifacts are lifeless exclusively from a reductionist biological perspective: in the material-semiotic compound of "storied matter" (1), *tirakuna* are animated by tales of encounters and transformations, catastrophes and survivals:

---

[45] "Reading Rancière through Mariano and Nazario's stories, the division between what is seen and heard in the sphere of politics (and what is not seen or heard) corresponds to a division between the historical and the ahistorical" (de la Cadena 2015, 278).

[46] On Rancière's theory of subjectivization and the postcolonial "politics of bodies," see Quintana (2020): "Rancière's way of thinking the forms of emancipation (individual and collective) challenges that subject and, with it, the humanist dispositif of person, with its rigid boundaries between the genuinely human, rational, capable of articulate language, and the bare life of a being doomed to mere survival, to impotence, or to the dispossession of its capacities for agency ... Rancière's formulations regarding what I have broadly called here a 'politics of bodies' can also be significant for reflecting on political agency today, in the times of late capitalism and its ways of *dispossessing* those it marginalizes, includes through exclusion, or abandons" (Quintana 2020, 5).

[47] Enrico Cesaretti has traced the characteristics of "elemental narratives" shaped, in the Italian context, by oil, marble, asbestos, steel, and concrete. These narratives occupy a middle place that "speak of our simultaneous (co)existence in both imaginative and material universes" (Cesaretti 2020, 3). On the nonanthropocentric narratives coproduced by dioxins and contamination, see also Seger (2022).

> Stories, both pre-Hispanic and contemporary, record the actions of the once and future animate Andean topography. In many of these stories, life-forms – both humans and animals – turn into rocks, while in others, stones animate. Not subject to death and decay, stone was life immobilized. It was animacy "paused" for an unspecified period. (Dean 2010, 5)

The middle place of storied matter is the terrain chosen by ethnographers that privilege thick descriptions of ritual enactments and mythical narratives (Chase 2015). In her conversations with the Turpos, de la Cadena embraces the semiotized landscape of Indigenous natures to build her chronicle of Andean earth-beings. *Tirakuna*'s subjectivity takes shape from *willakuys*, the Quechua word for stories: a *willakuy* consists in "the act of telling or narrating an event that happened, sometimes leaving topographic traces – a lagoon, a cliff, a rock formation – that make the event present" (de la Cadena 2015, 28). Stones and springs act with humans because the stories of the Turpos animate Andean natures through metaphoric ascriptions, biomorphisms, anthropomorphisms, and other modeling tools.[48] On this semiotic terrain, Quechua personifications of nonlife can be read against Western personhood: petrified ancestors, hungry stones, and speaking mountains are "dis-anthropocentric" devices "aimed at reducing the (linguistic, perceptive, and ethical) distance between the human and the nonhuman" (Iovino & Oppermann 2014, 8).[49] Instead of confirming Western prejudices about the essence of personhood and interiorities,[50] the stories of *tirakuna* delink geobodies from biocentrism.

We can now take a step beyond the political context chosen by de la Cadena. How can we account for ethnohistorical constellations in which *tirakuna* have made alliances with landscapes, animals, and humans outside of the logic of modern state politics? We owe to Catherine J. Allen an ethnographic tale of the genesis of a particular class of earth-beings, the tiny stone animals called *inqaychus*. These aree sexually undetermined miniature sculptures of domestic herd animals – llamas, alpacas, and sheep – that Andean shepherds believe are made and animated by mountains (Allen 2016a). In the small Quechua-speaking highland communities of Sonqo, in the department of Cuzco in southern Peru, these stony figures come to their petrified life in critical times and places: "cracks in the world's fabric, moments of opening with potential for change in scale configuration" (337). *Inqaychus* emerge from "water doors" and other loci of metamorphoses that coincide with cosmic turning points:

---

[48] On these narrative techniques of semiotization of matter, see Maran (2014, 151).

[49] Italo Calvino's speaking stone and the figure of speech of prosopopoeia are also disanthropocentric rhetorical devices.

[50] On interiority and personhood, see Descola (2005). For a critical assessment of Descola's notion of interiority, see the interview with Emmanuel Alloa and Lariana Larison (2020).

> During my visits to Sonqo I stayed with families who graciously let me
> participate in ritual activities which included the care and feeding of *inqaychus*.
> I learned that *inqaychus* emerge from marshy springs on the treeless slopes of
> Antaqaqa, Sonqo's guardian hill. The springs are "water doors" (*unu punku*)
> opening to an interior landscape within the hill. (333)

De la Cadena also refers to an *inqaychu* that, according to Nazario Turpo,
"Ausangate had made my father find" (de la Cadena 2015, 107). The Turpos
told de la Cadena that these stones are the "earth-being itself – a piece of it,
which is also all of it – but shaped in a specific form" (107). As *tirakuna*, they
are subjects that can be captured but not owned; they must be cared for, and also
respected in their autonomy, as also confirmed by Allen's native informants:

> Such remarkable things could not be of human manufacture. *Apukuna* (powerful
> places in the landscape) bestow *inqaychus* on favored individuals who then pass
> them on to their descendents through the generations. Shepherds in very high-
> altitude communities devoted to pastoralism say *inqaychus* are beautiful animals
> that emerge from springs and glacial lakes at night or in dense morning fog.
> A quick-witted individual who encounters such a creature can capture it by
> touching it with his foot or throwing a coca cloth over it ... Then the marvelous
> animal shrinks until it becomes a tiny stone, which should be bundled still warm
> and quivering inside the coca cloth and quickly carried home. Although the
> marvelous creature has been captured it is not "owned" but stays of its own
> accord. (Allen 2016a, 328)

Inqaychus are not defined by their relationship with the modern state. These
domestic *tirakuna* have become subjects by occupying, since their origins, an
incommensurable in-between whose name is *alqa*, "a Quechua word which
denotes rupture, change in direction or change in tonality" (337).

> *Alqa* is the singular switch-point where a thing leaves off being what it is and
> becomes something else ... *Alqa* is the point at which the slope of a hillside
> changes, or the ground is broken, defining a distinct protuberance ... *Alqa* is
> the place and moment of transformation, definition and identity. The first
> sunrise, when Inti blazed into existence, was *alqa* at a cosmic scale; so are the
> annual turning points in the Sun's orbit when the Earth is lively and marvel-
> ous herd animals emerge from the water doors – and if one is lucky, they turn
> to little stones. (337–8)

Alqa signifies these ambiguous, dangerous, and eventful space–times, fractures
of reality that correspond to generative events.[51] It is at these conjunctures that
lithification donates to *inqaychus* their suspended vitality:

---

[51] A seminal conjuncture of this kind is the *pachakuti*, the mythic apocalypse that "destroyed a pre-
human age of the world lit by a copper sun and populated by giants" (Allen 2016b, 425).

Water doors, themselves places of rupture, are sites of lithification. People as well as animals turn into stone there. In Sonqo, *inqaychus* are said to frequent a deep ravine where three streams meet in a turbulent encounter called *tinku*. I was warned strenuously never to go near this highly dangerous "water door" because giant felines and *amarus* (dragon-like serpents) emerge from the underworld there. The Incas are said to have passed through this ravine as they fled from the Spanish invaders and an Inca girl turned to stone when she lagged behind her companions to urinate. She is still there, spouting water near her base. The Inca girl's transformation is the converse of that undergone by *inqaychus*. Both are transformed around water and change dimension in the process; but *inqaychus* emerge from water and shrink as they turn to stone while the Inca Daughter enters water, "water" emerges from her, and she grows in size while turning to stone. Another immense stone girl (*sipas qaqa*) sits next to a mountain lake high in the grasslands above Sonqo. She, too, has a stream of water trickling from her base. It is said that she turned to stone while pausing to urinate during her flight from a doomed city. At that very moment a deluge flooded that city and became the lake. These are but two examples of lithification in an Andean landscape covered with people and animals transformed at moments/places of cosmic transition or rupture into gigantic boulders, hills, outcrops and even mountains. (338)

Inqaychus appear to ethnographers as "nested," "distributed," or "fractal" persons (Allen 2016b, 426). I approach them instead as beings incommensurable with the biocentric imaginary of Western personhood. They are shape-shifting natural subjects that acquire their identity at the crossroads of ontological transformations, in moments and places of passage. *Inqaychus* share with *tirakuna* a congealed genesis: they are pauses in the order of nature, the result of turbulent encounters and crises of presence. Since Andean earth-beings act on a geosocial stage that is not choreographed around the mask of the Latin *persona* (Mauss 1985, 14), their genesis offers an alternative paradigm of subject formation. Despite centuries of colonialism, in the Andean landscape of stones, *tirakuna* cross geological, biological, and historical planes, confounding life with nonlife. In the next section, I will show how stones have played a crucial role in defining subjectivity from the dawn of humanity, and how erratic boulders continue to trouble the Western architecture of human personhood.

3 Polemical Scenes

3.1 The Stone Substitute

Stones have never been a passive background to animal life. The manufacturing of flake tools, spears, hammerstones, and hand axes has marked hominization, the becoming human of our primate ancestors. Lambros Malafouris argues that an "archeology of the mind," an origin story of personhood, should begin with early humans' material engagement with the tools of the Stone Age: "it is familiar when the hand grasps a stone and makes it a tool, yet it remains *terra incognita* in that, despite a long genealogy of analytic efforts, just what this grasping implies for humans remains elusive and refuses to be reduced and read in the form of a linear evolutionary narrative" (Malafouris 2013, 15). Rethinking subjecthood from the vantage point of lithic encounters resets any preconception about the division of persons, bodies, and the world of objects.

Malafouris's archaeology of the mind relies on James Gibson's notion of "affordances," the cognitive manipulability of the environment by the animal (Gibson 2015, 120–35). Early stone tools shaped human perception and thought by allowing, constraining, and channeling a variety of feedbacks between matter and the mind. This, for Malafouris, is the middle zone in which the boundary between the subjective and the objective, "the mental and the physical collapses" (Malafouris 2013, 140). Each "given context of engagement" (144) enacts different types of material signs and unleashes distinct processes of projection, relations, and bodily skills. The lithic-hominid assemblages of the Stone Age set the pattern of what an "embodied mind" looks like: a component of an ecology in which humans coevolve through their engagements with matter and nonhumans.

This anthropology of primordial relations with nonlife offers seductive clues for shifting ecology away from standard evolutionary paradigms. And yet, we should be cautious. What role have earth-beings played in the archeology of the mind? Is there only one human mind, or does the decolonial pluralization of worlds affect the understanding of cognitive structures? For Gibson, there is only "one world," the world of affordances, a flat socioecological terrain blind to the heterogeneity of earth-beings and their subjectivities: "there is only one world, however diverse, and all animals live in it, although we human animals have altered it to suit ourselves ... we were created by the world we live in" (Gibson 2015, 121–2). In this one world of perception and action, humans alter the environment to accommodate their anthropological thirst; they bend natural affordances to the advantage of their species-specific goals:

> In the last few thousand years, as everybody now realizes, the very face of the earth has been modified by man. The layout of surfaces has been changed, by cutting, clearing, leveling, paving, and building. ... Why has man changed the shapes and substances of his environment? To change what it affords him. He has made more available what benefits him and less pressing what injures him. In making life easier for himself, of course, he has made life harder for most of the other animals. Over the millennia, he has made it easier for himself to get food, easier to keep warm, easier to see at night, easier to get about, and easier to train his offspring. (121–2)

My hypothesis is that earth-beings resist the standardizing effect of "mutual affordances" (127). As shown in Section 2, Andean *tirakuna* teach us that relationships are between incommensurable worlds, not within a unified planetary ecology of the mind. There can be no central locus of cognition if what is at stake are heterogeneous worldings, the right to define humanity and nature, subjectivity and objecthood. Are mountains subjects? Can stones listen? What form of presence should societies attribute to "a cliff face, a wall, a chasm, and a stream" that are perceived as barriers only because "they do not afford pedestrian locomotion unless there is a door, a gate, or a bridge?" (124).

Geobodies have inspired an astonishing variety of ritualizations and symbolizations because they do not favor human designs and are not attuned with our sensorium. Their existence can be perceived as an affordance but, in most cases, it is a *heteron*, the Greek term for an other, a nonself (Rancière 1992, 59). Stones persist and humans die, stones stand firm and animals wander. Rocks condense time into matter in ways that are precluded to biological actors: their strata are an archive of the forces that decompose and recompose life; in their solid space–time warps, the rhythms of creation and destruction of organisms, the contact zones between individual bodies and the environment become porous.[52] Geobodies favor animal life only partially: beyond these engagements, only creative relationships with their divergent existence can be devised.

The problem posed by the relative autonomy of nonlife – simultaneously an affordance of the animal and a refractory presence – has generated a diversity of solutions that represent as many socializations of geobodies. Let's consider aniconic rocks: they have accompanied daily life and ceremonial practices across the planet since the Neolithic as wishing and healing stones, dolmens, menhirs, capstones, and stone circles. The durability of rocks has made them monuments and "navels" of the Earth; the power of volcanism and earthquakes has spurred chthonic myths; the rarity, colors, luminescence, and properties of gems have fueled Arabic, Greek, Roman, and medieval books on stones, the lapidaries (Macrì 2009). Ancient traditions speculate on the singularity of lithic beings, on the aberrations, deformities, and spontaneous images imprinted on stones that punctuate the strata of the Earth.[53] Alchemy has placed the pursuit of a "philosopher's stone" at the core of its practices (Pinkus 2010). Petrified landscapes can be found or artfully made to reenact myths of origin. Rocks

---

[52] "The striations of rock that jut out over the sea not only mark time with their varied colors and lines, but *make* time through their encounters with the waves and wind" (Neimanis & Loewen Walker 2014, 569). On the poetics of the lithic, see Farrier (2019).

[53] See Jurgis Baltrusaitis's (1957) ontology of deformity and the Surrealist hermeneutics of lithic imagination (Caillois 1985). On this topic, see Coglitore (2004).

are semiotized by ritual practices, indexical connections, and metaphorical tropes: from Chinese geomancy and Zen Buddhist *karesansui* (dry landscapes) gardens in Japan, to Australian Dreamtime landscapes and megalithic cultures in Europe, they have been absorbed into cosmological and aesthetic systems, narratives of metamorphoses. In these ontological theaters, rocks act as energy-beings, puzzling witnesses, or deceptive traces of cosmic creations and power struggles.

Despite their material estrangement from biological life, stones inhabit narrative worlds in which they can be animated and switch place with the universe of living beings, acquiring movement, growth, emotions, social skills, and death. In the fourth century BC, Theophrastus's treatise on stones attributed, with some irony, "the greatest and most wonderful power" to stones that can "give birth to young" and reproduce themselves (Theopfrastus 1956, 46). The *Physiologus*, the second century AD Hellenistic model of medieval bestiaries, lists as subjects not only plants and animals but also rocks of "masculine and feminine gender" (Curley 1979, 6), as well as moving stones such as the agate, which when it "comes to the pearl, it stops and does not move" (34). In Japan, rocks can contain spirits (*kami*), receive gendered connotations, and be wedded, as *Meoto Iwa*, the married rocks off the northern coast of the Itoshima Peninsula, which are bound by a thick ceremonial rope. Stones also continue to find their way back if they are removed, as the "homing stones" of Ireland (Zucchelli 2016, 87), or they grow if they are buried in the attempt to eradicate pagan rites. In England,

> in 1858, the antiquarian William Long visited Avebury to take an inventory of the site and observed that people here "adopt the belief (to which they cling most pertinaciously) that *stones grow.*" If stones, like plants, had come from the Earth, their burial was also a replanting, "a returning of the sarsens to their place of origin," much as a human burial is also a return: an end, a beginning, and a moment in an always unfinished process. (Raffles 2020, 71).

These kaleidoscopic engagements with the lithic world have been framed by researchers within the evolution of the mind and the invention of sociotechnical systems: the history of magic, divination, and medicine, and the sociology of judicial and political rituals. The third ecology has a different aim: it is concerned with the scenes in which nonlife stages its own political subjectivity and confronts humans (and gods) with its modes of existence, redefining regimes of inhabitation of the Earth, altering distributions of natures, identities, bodies, and humanity.

The political ecology of nonlife allows us to interpret also ancient lithic sites, such as the *omphalos* ("navel") of Delphi. This stone was believed by the ancient

Figure 2 Rhea presenting the stone substitute to Cronus. Drawing from the bas-relief of a Roman altar. Wikimedia Commons. https://bit.ly/467XTjc.

Greeks to be at the center of the Earth, and served as the most powerful site of communication between gods and humans, the Delphic Oracle.[54] The *omphalos* is a specimen of the *baetyli*, the sacred stones of Mediterranean antiquity, which stood at the core of Semitic, Phoenician, Greek, and Roman cults. These were also exceptional geological entities: erratic boulders, rare rocks (agate, basalts), geophysical formations, and remains of meteorites, as most likely the black stone of the Kaaba, in Mecca. In the *Theogony* (8th–7th century BC), Hesiod associates the *omphalos* of Delphi with the stone that Cronus mistakes for his son Zeus (see Figure 2). His account of the deception of Cronus offers a master narrative for a political understanding of lithic beings. Cronus is aware that one of his children will oust him from power and tries unsuccessfully to evade his fate by devouring them. Thanks to a stone, Gaia and Ouranos cheat Cronus and protect Zeus, Rhea's child, from his father's cannibalism (Davidson 1995). They secretly rear Zeus in Crete and help Rhea substitute her son with a stone disguised as the child: instead of Zeus, Cronus

---

[54] The Oracle of Delphi, enshrined from the eighth century BC in a temple dedicated to Apollo, is where the priestess Pythia delivered her prophecies. An engraved oval marble stone, now exhibited at the Archaeological Museum of Delphi, was found at the sanctuary and is believed to be a Hellenistic copy of the original *omphalos* stone. The Apollonian temple replaced an archaic site of divination, presided by chthonic cults. Stone navels often had phallic or egg shapes, in association with ancient cults of fertility.

swallows a rock wrapped in swaddling cloth. This deception allows Zeus to survive and overthrow his father Cronus, thus inaugurating his Olympian reign:

> For he [Cronus] had learned from Gaia and from starry Ouranos / that his own child [Zeus] would conquer him, powerful though he was / . . . and swallowed up his children . . . / But to the son of Ouranos, the older gods' great lord,/ a huge rock wrapped in swaddling clothes she gave to be devoured./ He took it in his hand and in his belly crammed it down, / not knowing that he 'd swallowed rock/. (Hesiod 2006, 37–8)

Zeus then induces Cronus to vomit the stone, his brothers, and his sisters, and places the stone on the slopes of the Mount Parnassus, where Delphi's sanctuary is located: "And first he [Cronus] vomited up the stone, since last he gulped it down: / Zeus fixed it firm up on the broad-pathed earth and set it on / Holy Pytho, under Parnassus, in a hollow glen / to be a sign hereafter, a marvel for death-born men" (Hesiod 2006, 38). The Greek geographer Pausanias (second century AD) informs us that the stone is looked after in Delphi as a real child, "olive oil is poured over it each day and that at every festival unworked wool is placed on it" (Davidson 1995, 367).

Whereas the dispositif of the *persona* unifies the body and the soul in a living unity, the stone substitute initiates a polemical scene, it brings out "the contradiction between two logics" (Rancière 1999, 41). Hesiod's narrative stages lithic–human exchanges that coincide with the power struggle between the Titans and Zeus, the crucial political transition in Greek mythology. Oiled like a baby and covered with a woolen cloth, as Rhea did with the substitute stone that defeated Cronus's plans, Delphi's *omphalos* is perceived as a human infant. However, masked by its clothed personhood is the political subjectivity of a lithic being, a stone that affirms a difference with the chthonic order of the Titans. The *omphalos* is a paradoxical presence that congeals the difference between two regimes of existence: it is at the same time an ordinary stone, an infant, and a sacred being. For this reason it is the site of the Oracle, where the communication between humans and gods took place, because it is in itself a transitional object, constituted during an ancient war of the worlds, where two regimes of power crossed paths. There is no animation and vitality in Hesiod's account of the mythical origin of Delphi's *omphalos*. The stone substitute is a lifeless earth-being that initiated a new distribution of the sensible in a tragicomedy of cheating and emancipation.

To understand the distinctive material presence of the *omphalos*, we can borrow the notion of "new monument" from contemporary art practices. Reflecting on the large minimalist artworks of Donald Judd, Robert Morris, Sol Le Witt, and Dan Flavin, the land-art artist Robert Smithson saw in their work an unprecedented aesthetic scene and form of monumentality: "new monuments ... not built for the ages, but rather against the ages" (Smithson 1979, 11). In these material objects, "time as decay or biological evolution" had been eliminated and temporality had become "a place minus motion," an odd stasis (11). The *omphalos*'s material presence is such a new monument: a stone takes part in a passage of power that is also a shift in the cultural arrangement of the world. Dressed up and oiled, it takes on a strange monumentality – deceptively for Cronus and ceremonially for the followers of the Olympian gods. The stone undergoes a transformation into an earth-being that freezes time, dodging biological evolution through its materiality, standing against the ages. Set in stone is a Greek variant of the Quechua *alqa*: a petrification of the conjuncture in which things are not what they used to be and have become something else, other subjects.

3.2 Erratics

Navel stones could be skillfully shaped and carved or they could retain their original formless consistency, as in the case of Aill na Míreann, the Stone Navel of Ireland, a twenty-foot-tall erratic boulder in County Westmeath, whose social role "dates back into the earliest time of human activity in Ireland" (Zucchelli 2016, 10). Aill na Míreann reminds us that, among geobodies, erratic boulders – from the Latin *errare*, to wander – stand out as mavericks of their environments. Transported by glaciers and tsunamis, they have lost their geological homeland. With their eccentric geophysical location in valleys, plains, and hills detached from mountains and rocks of similar mineral composition, these out-of-place rocks have functioned as natural perceptual riddles that afford only confusing engagements and divergent interpretations. Across continents, they have been carved with petroglyphs, used for fertility rites, associated with ancestors and spirits, or condemned by Catholic extirpators of idols such as Bishop Saint Maximus of the Diocese of Turin (408–23 AD), who "hurled invectives against the rocks of the devil's altars" (Motta 2007, 317). For millennia, when they were not yet rare scientific curiosities to be rescued from the stone-thirsty construction industry,[55] the enigmatic presence of erratic boulders has inspired ritual practices, myths, and legends. Before modern glaciology, erratics stirred diluvialist theories and Biblical interpretations of earth history (Rudwick 2008).[56]

---

[55] Erratics are now also collected in rock gardens, zoos of inanimate nature: "collections of erratic boulders are created mainly to preserve and protect these silent witnesses of the glacial periods and to provide the opportunity to meet human needs in terms of learning about the region's inanimate natural heritage" (Górska-Zabielska 2021).

[56] Contemporary creationist movements are still recurring to "flood geology" to prove the occurrence of the Biblical Deluge (Whitcomb and Morris 1961). Flood theory appeals also to

Like Neolithic standing stones and their sci-fi reenactments,[57] the semiotic poverty and isolation of erratics have continued to encourage the conjectures of practitioners of stone-cults, archeoastronomy, esotericism, geomagnetism, and speculative cosmologies.[58]

From the perspective of the third ecology, erratics provide evidence in support of Rancière's hypothesis that "a process of subjectivization is a process of disidentification" (Rancière 1992, 61). These rocks have received subjective connotations – as spirits, messengers, petrified ancestors – because they have been stripped from their geological contexts by ancient planetary traumas. They have lost their morphological environments and they now dwell in our historical time as relics of natural history's crises. As isolated fragments of geological ages, they became disidentified from their landscapes. Their materiality appears as a ruin in the Earth's ruthless metamorphoses, a mode of existence suspended between ancient catastrophes and their contemporary presence.

The Pierre des Marmettes is a 1,800 cubic meter glacial boulder, surrounded by concrete and vineyards, and overseeing the Rhône valley in the Swiss Alps (see Figure 3).[59] This uncanny location near the village of Monthey, which is now the construction site of a hospital's parking lot, was reached 15,000 years ago, at the end of the Last Ice Age, after a journey of thirty kilometers initiated ·on Mont Blanc. The block of granite has been detached from its geological nursery by the retreat of the Rhône glacier, which 20,000 years ago covered most of southwestern Switzerland and is currently reduced to a seventeen-square-kilometer mass of melting grey ice, partially covered by white polyester blankets to slow its disappearance.[60]

Whereas other erratic stones in the Alps show traces of ancient petroglyphs and are endowed with religious and archaeological connotations, the Pierre des Marmettes is a large but marginal earth-being, a scarred rock left behind by the moraine of Monthey-Collombey. On top of it, an abandoned hut with

---

mainstream media; see the Netflix pseudo-scientific documentary *Ancient Apocalypse* (2022), presented by Graham Hancock.

[57] "Neolithic standing stones 'challenge archaeological interpretation,' admit the archaeologists Adrian Challands, Mark Edmonds, and Colin Richards. 'As single or paired examples,' they write, 'they rest in isolated unfathomable splendour.' Standing stones invite speculation – demand it, even – but they offer few answers to the questions they pose" (Raffles 2020, 57). A standing stone appearing as an alien subject and time-machine is the monolith of Stanley Kubrick's *2001: A Space Odyssey* (see also the novel by Clarke [1968]).

[58] See Immanuel Velikovsky's (1955) planetary catastrophism and flood theories.

[59] The origin of its name is uncertain: it could derive from monsieur Mermet, the name of the eighteenth-century owner of the granite block (Bernard, Reynard, & Jacob 2013).

[60] D. Finch-Race & S. Hochleithner (2021), Rhone Glacier and the Eisgrotte (https://unrulyna tures.ch/Rhone-Glacier-and-the-Eisgrotte).

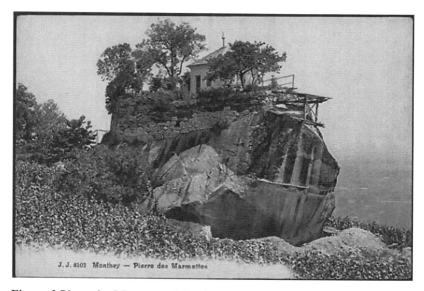

Figure 3 Pierre des Marmettes, Monthey, Switzerland. Postcard, 1905. Public domain.

a fireplace reminds us of the days when the erratic was inhabited and used as a lookout. As a convenient source of valuable granite placed near cities and easily accessible, erratic blocks in the central plateau of Switzerland were used in the nineteenth century for stone extraction and rapidly disappeared. The Pierre des Marmettes was also destined to this fate, which explains why what is left of it is shaped geometrically: parts of its body were cut away by Italian immigrant workers and transfigured into the peristyles adorning the Church of Monthey.

Since the late eighteenth century, Alpine erratic boulders have also served as geologic informants: by attending to the mineral composition of the Pierre des Marmettes and other erratics, Jean de Charpentier demonstrated their glacial origin and convincingly proved the past extension and retreat stages of major Alpine glaciers, a milestone in the nineteenth-century development of glaciology (Charpentier 1841).[61] "Around 1850, erratic blocks were recognized, with moraines and glacial striae, as the principal indices used for the reconstruction of former alpine glaciers" (Reynard 2004, 26), and scientists began to challenge extraction companies, publicly advocating for the preservation of

---

[61] Agassiz's (2012) *Etudes sur les glaciers* (1840) expanded on Charpentier's work, arguing that a single vast ice sheet had in fact covered much of the continent. These hypotheses were seminal in the development of a widely accepted theory of glaciation (Hutton 2013, 115). Research on the erratics of the Valais helped geologists introduce the new paradigm of the Ice Age and brought to an end the old diluvial theory (Woodward 2014, 30).

erratics with a petition published in national and international newspapers (Favre & Studer 1867). In 1905, the private owner of the Pierre des Marmettes sold it to quarries. Concerned with the survival of their local earth-being, citizens joined naturalists, the city of Monthey, and the cantonal authority in a significant financial effort: the Swiss Society for Natural Research eventually acquired the block at twice its market price, paying CHF 31,500 to the rock owner (Bernard, Reynard, & Jacob 2013). That mobilization led to the establishment of the Swiss Commission for Nature Protection (SNK), the first Swiss environmental society.

The Pierre des Marmettes owes its peculiar temperament to its allochthonous origin and perceptual intractability (Figure 4). It is unmistakably out of place – spatially, temporally, and ecologically. A geological intruder, it hosts on its top a curious Alpine garden nested around the crumbling hut, a micro-habitat sustained by its acid crystalline rock, at odds with the surrounding flora. From geologists in search of its origins, to locals protecting their celebrity and tourists attracted by this curiosity of natural history, it has continued to be a perturbation in the ecosystems and landscapes. Severed from its geological hotbed, carried away by a moraine, quarried, studied, protected, and now abandoned in a parking lot, the Pierre des Marmettes continues to undergo subjectivizations. It is a quiet rock as well as a restless earth-being.

Figure 4 The Pierre des Marmettes (2022). Photo by the author.

Erratics materialize ruptures. They are fragments of deep time that exist in between temporal regimes. From their ancient mobility, they derive the power to confound the morphology of landscapes and to unsettle political boundaries, as in the case of the massive boulders "found on German plains originating in Scandinavia, in Brandenburg from across the Baltic Sea, and in St. Petersburg from somewhere near Finland" (Hutton 2013, 114). Doreen Massey (2005) tells us the story of "Hamburg's Oldest Immigrant," a 217-ton erratic boulder detached 400,000 years ago from present-day southern Sweden and carried by glaciers to its present location in Germany. Accidentally discovered in the Elbe River in 1999, at a depth of fifteen meters, it soon became a symbol for immigrants' rights:

> In the autumn of 1999 workers labouring on the bed of the Elbe River where it begins to open out to the sea at Hamburg came up against a massive boulder. It was a noteworthy event and made the news. The rock became popular and the people of Hamburg began to visit it. But this celebrated resident of the city turned out to be an immigrant. It is an erratic, pushed south by the ice thousands of years ago and left here as the ice retreated. By no means, then, a "local" boulder. (Massey 2005, 149)

The Hamburg erratic has displaced the social perception of place and identity: its massive body is at the same time a local presence and a migrant, it arrived from across the sea but is firmly rooted in the city. Soon, the boulder became the centerpiece of a campaign for the legalization of immigrants in Hamburg, featured on posters as a symbol of hybrid identities mixing seafaring and steadiness, otherness, and familiarity (150).

Erratic boulders bring us back to Rancière's theory of political subjectivization, the cornerstone of de la Cadena's reading of Andean *tirakuna* as earth-beings. They prove Rancière's key intuition: political subjectivities presuppose "paradoxical scenes" (Rancière 1999, 41). Erratics in the Swiss Alps and in the bed of the Elbe River assert their natural subjectivity and unsettle the perception of the environment, even if they are not ritualistically addressed by Indigenous societies. As minor earth-beings, these wanderers have been captured by geological turmoil, extractions, environmental anxieties, and migration imaginaries. Haunted by human and geological forces and left behind by immense glaciers, the Pierre des Marmettes and the Hamburg erratic have survived weathering and granite quarrying, witnessing commodification and infrastructural projects. In their new lands, subjectivization followed disidentification: they have been personified as informants and immigrants, they inspired conservation movements and immigration rights, they hosted fragile micro-ecosystems and revealed their ancient metamorphoses to the scientific community.

Contemporary artists have captured the lithic subjectivity of boulders. Their works reveal traces of their origins in turning points of natural and social history. Jeffrey Jerome Cohen defines this condition as "intra-catastrophe," the sensed experience of participating in metamorphic critical events, planetary crises of presence: "Rocks ... index the extinctions of remote epochs, extinctions that near again. They yield narratives of celestial fire, massive volcanic blasts, an atmosphere inimical to life, an earth gripped by ice, ablaze, overheated, engulfed in sudden flood" (Cohen 2015, 63).

The video installation *Tsunami Boulder Project* (2015–), by the Japanese artist Motoyuki Shitamichi, brings the viewer to the Miyako and Yaeyama Islands, a remote archipelago in the southwestern area of Okinawa Prefecture, where gigantic boulders were uprooted from their seabed during catastrophic tsunamis (Figure 5). Geologists have paid attention to this evocative landscape, a still life of geological shape-shifting vicissitudes. Massive isolated boulders of non-glacial origin can be found along beaches, reefs, and lowlands of the Atlantic, Pacific and Indian oceans. They were displaced from the seabed by tsunamis or storm waves and deposited on coastlines. The most striking tsunami boulders, the southern Ryukyu Islands, were washed ashore by the 1771 Meiwa Tsunami. Many of them have sedimentary or coralline compositions and have

Figure 5 Motoyuki Shitamichi, *Tsunami Boulder Project* (2021), Museum of Contemporary Art, Tokyo, Japan. Courtesy of the artist. The catalogue of the exhibition *Cosmo-Eggs* at the 2019 Venice Biennale included this project (Hattori et al. 2019).

become the host of seabirds and other species. On the Miyako Islands, locals have personalized them with nicknames (see Goto, Kawana, & Imamura 2010).

Shitamichi's large black-and-white videos document, with simultaneous projections, several hours in the daily (non)life of these boulders. Shitamichi's work meditates on the personalizations of erratics. Framed at the center of the video shots, the tsunami boulders' irregular and scarred rocky bodies are met by swarms of humans and nonhumans: migratory bird colonies and goats, tourists, fishermen, and farmers (Randerson 2022, 5–6). We are confronted by shy protagonists of a minor natural history: patient, silent, but also receptive and malleable mineral subjects that dwell on beaches, in forests, and on agricultural land, where they mingle with the sea, the weather, and the land, modifying their surfaces to host tropical vegetation, soil, guano, seashells, moss, birds, goats, and ropes.

There is nothing sacred in these other-than-human beings; they are found existences that lack a ritualized cultural history. Even so, they are overdetermined as subjects: Shitamichi's video camera discloses their nonlife, suspended between the past geological traumas that brought them to the islands and the present encounters with humans and nonhumans. Critical theory struggles to conceptualize the space–time that transforms stones into ecopolitical subjects, the sphere of reality in which the slow geophysical existence of the mineral world is reconfigured by sudden cataclysms of natural and social history. Instead, in Shitamichi's videos the contraction of multiple histories and times into singular geobodies becomes tangible. These lithic beings are cognitive and cultural outsiders that demonstrate the impossibility of constructing personhood through stable identifications: they are a fisherman's landmark, a site of folk religion, a historical landmark, they meet groups of schoolchildren and workers.[62]

Julian Charrière is a multimedia French-Swiss artist who conjures up geomorphic forces and geophysical identities, reenacting natural processes in surprising scenes.[63] His work takes us to remote locations – volcanoes, deserts, ice fields, undersea, and radioactive sites – as well as to museums and public spaces, where Charrière problematizes viewers' perception of nature in a time of planetary crisis. His work crosses deep time and current ecological concerns, enhancing and questioning the geoscientific construction of geobodies.

Not All Who Wander Are Lost (2019–) is a disorienting *Wunderkammer*, an environmental installation that functions as a "cabinet of geological curiosities," a space of wonder in which viewers experience nature as "a ruin in state

---

[62] Motoyuki Shitamichi, Tsunami Boulder (http://m-shitamichi.com/work/tsunami-boulder/).

[63] Julian Charrière, artist website (https://julian-charriere.net/).

Figure 6 Julian Charrière, *Not All Who Wander Are Lost* (2019). Intallation view, *Towards No Earthly Pole*, MASI Lugano, Lugano, Switzerland (2019). © the artist 2023, ProLitteris, Zurich. Photo by Jens Ziehe.

of flux" (Steer 2016) (Figure 6). Here, perforated erratic boulders that sit on their own drilled core samples, with inserted metal elements, stage a perplexing presence. What are these stones doing? Why are they hollowed? Charrière repurposes the mining technology of core sampling, which is used in quarrying and geological research. He excavates stone cylinders and places them under the pierced rocks. The planetary events that detached erratics from their source and set them in motion across landscapes are mimicked by this extractive technology. This results in bizarre conveyor belts, inducing in viewers the impression of a sliding of the erratics that continues *motu proprio* the original geological motion caused by glaciers. But now, it is human intervention and not geological history that consumes and breaks down the boulders, displacing them from their location and initiating their movement. By artificially reproducing a natural process, Charrière reactivates the decomposition and mobility of these stones. Deep history is prolonged into the present.

With its violent perforations, *Not All Who Wander Are Lost* denounces the plundering of mineral resources and the destruction of geobodies. At the same time, these hollowed boulders have become lighter and the extracted cones are now covered with precious metals. As the title of this work suggests, these rocks are wanderers, outsiders, but they are not lost: drilling has revealed their inner tendency to shift state and be something else, somewhere else, experimenting with motion in place. In Charrière's magical diorama, stones have become earth-beings, asserting the logic of lithic subjectivity and recapturing the forces of destruction, reinventing movement from within extinction, traveling on their own mutilated bodies. We are witnessing the subjectivity of beings that endure at the intersection of movement and stasis, destruction and self-reliance. In them, passivity is a promise of emancipation, a scandal for the neoliberal order of nature.

3.3 Being Possessed

The Pierre des Marmettes, the Hamburg erratic, the *Tsunami Boulder Project*, and Charrière's perforated stones are immersed in forces that they cannot master. By being what they are where they are, by weathering and surviving glaciers, tsunamis, extractions, and drillings, they have acquired their distinct appearance. These rocks are neither objects nor persons, neither inert nor alive. I have interpreted this unsettling presence as a puzzling subjectivization. But we should differentiate the ecopolitical subjectivity of geobodies from the "vibrant" aliveness of matter advocated by Jane Bennett (2009) and "vital materialists." For them, things are lively because they are endowed with nonhuman agency, "trajectories, propensities, or tendencies of their own" (Bennett 2009, viii). Bennett celebrates the "thing-power" of electricity, food, trash, and metal in the register of an impersonal life, of the vital materialities that "flow through and around us," of "the nonhuman powers circulating around and within human bodies" (x). Nothing escapes the activity and creativity of animated things of all sorts, the currents of experience of nonhuman bodies that can "destroy, enrich or disable, ennoble or degrade us" (ix).

   The pitfall of this material vitalism is that it rests on the notion of agency. Agency allows Bennett to multiply exponentially and spread to nonliving beings the paradigm of personhood, including its supposed vitality, autonomy, creativity, and emancipative tendencies: "I believe that encounters with lively matter can . . . expose a wider distribution of agency, and reshape the self and its interests" (122). I concur instead with Tim Ingold: it is "perverse" to postulate the existence of an agency of humans and then extend it to nonhumans (Ingold 2013, 96).[64] This supposition radically simplifies the forces of individuation and does not recognize how geobodies can, at the same time, be subjective and passive:

---

[64] "Assuming that persons are capable of acting because they possess an agency, the question was one of how objects in the vicinity of these persons could nevertheless 'act back', causing them to do what they otherwise might not. The facile answer was to say that the objects, too, possess agency" (Ingold 2013, 96).

> That all living beings, humans included, are forever "immersed in action" – as
> the philosopher Alfred North Whitehead once put it – from the moment of
> birth if not before, is not in doubt. All are at sea in the tumult. However, to
> attribute this action to an agency, of which it is supposed to be the effect,
> seems like putting everything back to front. (96)

Humans and nonhumans do not act because they possess an imaginary principle
of autonomy. Only retrospectively, and through many problematic reductions, can
we trace actions back to a "putative point of origin" and attribute to it the
ownership of an agency. In reality, "humans do not *possess* agency; nor, for that
matter, do non-humans. They are rather possessed by action" (97). If we follow
Ingold and abandon individualized agencies, we can reclaim the specificity of
lithic subjectivity without falling into the trap of biologism. Erratics are subjects
even if their matter is not sentient, agentic, lively, and vibrant. Political subjectivization emerges from geobodies possessed by plural forms of action, when their
situatedness exposes the drama that affects them. Earth-beings cannot escape the
actions that scar, plunder, extract, and degrade them; this theatre of domination is
their environment, the world in which they are immersed. And yet, in this collapse
of agency, they stand out as subjects, they interrogate our understanding of life
and action, of personhood and relations.

Bennett's vitalism has popularized a monadological tradition that, from
Leibniz to Deleuze, has subjectivized nature and extended individuality to stones
and germs, technologies, galaxies, and plants (Debaise 2017b). For this radical
naturalism, there are only subjects interacting with each other, objects are nothing
other than subjects possessed by other subjects.[65] Deleuze's rehabilitation of
Whitehead's notion of "prehension" lies at the core of this paradigm (Debaise
2017a), which has the serious drawback of being unable to pull subjectivity apart
from life. Either geobodies are alive or they are not subjects:

> Prehension is individual unity. . . . an element is the given, the "datum" of another
> element that prehends it . . . Everything prehends its antecedents and its concomi-
> tants and, by degrees, prehends a world. The eye is a prehension of light. Living
> beings prehend water, soil, carbon, and salts. At a given moment the pyramid
> prehends Napoleon's soldiers . . . We can say that "echoes, reflections, traces,
> prismatic deformations, perspective, thresholds, folds" are prehensions that
> somehow anticipate psychic life. (Deleuze 1993, 78)

---

[65] Debaise distinguishes the ontological formulation of agency and possession, his "speculative empiri-
cism," from legal and political forms of appropriation: "the possessive agency should not be confused
with the action of 'taking possession' of an object by a subject. This would lead to a reduction of the
dynamics of power to simple power relationships. Instead, the agency is essentially immaterial and
inductive, which is pointed out by notions such as 'influence', 'sympathy', 'imitation', 'attraction'
and 'magnetism'" (Debaise 2008, 5). From the viewpoint of the third ecology, the ontologies of
possession are a concrescence of the legal and social matrix of personhood as patrimonial ownership.

In Deleuze's reading, individual unity is the outcome of a universe of captures, living beings emerge from possessive relations. It is life that singularizes matter, not matter that deactivates life.

Works from the Global South tell us other stories. Regina José Galindo is a Guatemalan performance artist and poet who has created unsettling dramatizations of colonial violence.[66] The context of her performance *Piedra* (2013) is the genocide of Indigenous communities in Guatemala, in 36 years of terror that killed 200,000 people and stripped them of their land and livelihoods.[67] At the University of São Paulo, the audience is invited to participate in the "becoming stone" of Galindo's body.[68] Covered with charcoal and immobile as a lithic being, Galindo's social personhood is disintegrated as spectators urinate on her body, reenacting gendered violence: "My body remains immobile, covered with charcoal. Two volunteers and someone from the audience urinate on the stone-body" (Galindo, in Iovino 2017, 190). A poem accompanies the artist's metamorphosis into an earth-being: "I am a stone / I don't feel the beatings / humiliation / lascivious stares / other bodies over mine / hate. / I am a stone / in me / the history of the world" (Galindo 2017, 198).

The actions of the volunteers and the gazes of the audience strip Galindo of all humanity and vitality, reminding the viewers that life is not the natural habitat of bodies trapped in colonial territories. Through debasement, a disturbing subjectivization occupies the scene: Galindo is now a stone-being, a cosmic subject. Her poem clarifies how geobodies exceed the logic of possession and dispossession, the dialectic of Western personhood that requires "the essential indistinction … of subjectivization and subjection" (Esposito 2012b, 21). Violence has expelled her body but has also liberated it from the constraints of personhood.[69] In this landscape of deanimation, the lithic and the human are exchangeable subject-positions, allowing Galindo to metamorphose into an earth-being of the third ecology, lifeless but subjective: "I am a stone." Her performance denounces the predation of land and bodies, opposing it with the *mise-en-scène* of an earth-being. *Piedra* joins the lithic existence of Andean *tirakuna*; it is an *omphalos* for the age of terricides,[70]

---

[66] R. J. Galindo, artist website (www.reginajosegalindo.com/en/home-en/ www.reginajosega lindo.com/en/home-en/).

[67] See R. J. Galindo, *Piedra* (2013) (www.reginajosegalindo.com/piedra/) and the video of the performance (https://vimeo.com/groups/152383/videos/194496054).

[68] See L. Mengesha, *Piedra* by R. J. Galindo (https://hemisphericinstitute.org/en/emisferica-102/ 10-2-review-essays/piedra.html).

[69] Galindo & Murphy Turner (2021).

[70] The Movimiento de Mujeres Indigenas por el Buen Vivir defines terricide as "the killing of tangible ecosystems, the spiritual ecosystem, and that of the *pueblos* and of all forms of life" (Escobar, Osterweil, & Sharma 2022). On the Movimiento de Mujeres Indigenas por el Buen

which affirms the enigmatic subjectivity of nonlife: "I am a stone / in me / the history of the world."

4 The Invisible Landfill

4.1 Toxic Gardens

I ask the reader to travel 100 kilometers west of the Pierre des Marmettes to the small municipality of Onex, a few bus stops from the center of Geneva. Here, at the site of the Nant des Grandes-Communes, you will see a low-income suburban housing complex and the picturesque family gardens, "La Caroline," where residents cultivate their flowers and vegetables. What you probably don't know is that you are standing on a massive but invisible landfill (Figure 7).[71] Nothing special captures the sight; however, some metal fencing and scattered pumping installations near the wooden sheds suggest a problematic existence.

Figure 7 Family gardens, "La Caroline," installed on the landfill site of Nant des Grandes-Communes, Onex, Switzerland. Image by Stéphanie Girardclos.

Vivir, see Mendoza (2021). Achille Mbembe, inspired by Frantz Fanon's phenomenology of colonial violence, calls this colonial logic of destruction a "necropolitics" (Mbembe 2019).

[71] The subterranean landfill is made visible through an academic paper (Girardclos 2019), a few news articles (Jan-Hess 2016; Zumbach 2019), and administrative records (Conseil Municipal Genève 2003).

When the dump for Geneva's domestic waste in the peninsula of Aïre reached its maximum capacity, local authorities decided to open a landfill on this plot, which used to be a valley, filling this geobody with 270,000 cubic meters of trash:

> As of 1956, the state counsellor J. Dutoit, in charge of the Department of Public Works, takes steps to find a place to bury the city's waste. At the time, he obtains the authorization of the commune of Onex and owners of the site to create a "sludge dump", i.e. to fill in the Nant des Grandes-Communes, which is an elongated depression occupied by a small torrent (*nant*) outflowing into the Rhône River. The Administrative Counsel of the City of Geneva approves the construction of this new landfill. (Girardclos 2019, 2)

The valley changed its morphology and served until 1962 as the burial site for Geneva's, Onex's, and Lancy's solid waste.[72] Once filled up and flattened, the old landfill was reconditioned in 1962 and covered up with a silty-clay sediment 2–3 meters thick to limit the infiltration of water and the propagation of putrid smells, and the family gardens "La Caroline" were built on its surface.

I interpret this site as a European earth-being, representative of the dilemmas of the third ecology. The valley has lost its original geological features and yet its mode of existence cannot be reduced exclusively to an artificial dump. It survives as a hybrid socioecological being, a geobody that holds together the contradiction between geophysical processes, livability, and waste disposal. At first glance, this plot is reassuring. Swiss earth-beings have acquired a banal politeness and do not inspire awe as Andean *tirakuna* do. Their naturalness is reduced to functional buildings, managed landfills, and a tamed horticulture, the shy vegetables and flowers growing in the family gardens, on top of the invisible landfill. But earth-beings are not easy to contain. Despite the reconditioning of the site, a study describes the risks associated with the presence of methane gas: "Urgent security measures were defined and communicated to the owner of family gardens in May 1999, followed by a letter to the President of the Geneva Federation of family gardens in which the security measures to be applied to diminish but not completely dispel the risk of explosion were described" (5). The landfill's sanitation lasted until 2005: an intricate grid of pipes, fourteen wells, and pumping devices now try to collect the leachates pouring in the Rhône and capture the constant methane emissions, subjecting them to thermal oxidation. The challenge faced by the engineers was to harness the disobedient

---

[72] I became acquainted with this landfill in February 2019, thanks to an on-site visit led by Stéphanie Girardclos, in the context of the workshop "Beyond recycling: crossed perspectives on the management of waste, remains and surplus," Geneva, February 5, 2019. I am grateful to Stéphanie Girardclos and Valeria Wagner for allowing me to consult their paper before it became publicly available (Girardclos 2019, 14).

dynamism of 270,000 cubic meters of undegraded substances lying just underneath.[73] Sanitation did not come without economic reward: the land is privately owned and yet taxpayers contributed 85 percent of the CHF 2.8 million required for the remediation of the landfill. After a change in zoning rules, the cleaner state of the site allowed for the construction on this wounded valley of the residential buildings of Les Jardins d'Onex (Conseil Municipal de Genève 2003).

Today, besides vegetables and apartments, metal pipes are piercing the terrain of the family gardens, penetrating the landfill under the supervision of disciplined workers wearing helmets and uniforms. A commercial website reveals how the anonymous grey constructions built on the landfill are a compulsive assortment of technological devices that coexist with methane and leachates:

> The poor quality of the soil required special precautions. The building is thus founded on piles and protected by a self-contained degasification system ... A network of pipes circulates under a waterproof basement and a continuous ventilation system blows air into it, in order to repel and oxidize the methane gas likely to be emitted by the landfill's constituent materials. In addition, the exhaust pipes and basement walls were carefully sealed to prevent uncontrolled migration of methane gas, while a safety chimney was installed on the roof of the building.[74]

What remains invisible are the poisoning substances escaping the metal grid, and their afterlife in the lungs of the families growing vegetables and picnicking on the landfill.

Despite engineering and speculation, the private owners of the plot are still worried by the high maintenance costs of this environmental hazard. For this reason, beginning in 2025, 380 new housing units and an elementary school will be built on the poisonous valley, replacing the family gardens.[75] The expense of landfill management will be borne by public funding and the children of Onex will study and play on waste in an advanced state of decomposition: "A new school complex with a gym will be built, replacing the old one at 'Les Tattes', on the current family gardens and with new pedestrian pathways. The family gardens will be partly recreated on the site. Housing and shops will be built in place of the current demolished school."[76] Students will breathe methane and other gasses

---

[73] A historical document shows that there was also a significant use of chemical substances, allegedly DDT, to fight flies, which may have altered the process of decomposition of organic waste (Girardclos 2019, 4).

[74] Les Jardins d'Onex, Architectes.ch (www.architectes.ch/fr/reportages/logements/les-jardins-d-onex-61945), my translation.

[75] République et canton de Genève, Onex – Moraines du Rhône (www.ge.ch/dossier/nouveaux-quartiers/projets-quartier-rive-gauche/onex-moraines-du-rhone).

[76] Ibid.

that the local experts advising the developers consider harmless: "dozens of families grow vegetables there, without any problem, according to the gardeners and especially the various analysis reports," reassures the Geneva daily newspaper *Tribune de Genève* (Jan-Hess 2016).

4.2 A Strange Holobiont?

The small valley where the creek used to outflow into the Rhône is now inhabited by the invisible landfill. The Nant des Grandes-Communes has become an infrastructural earth-being, it serves as the receptacle of waste and the foundation of residential buildings and schools. For the neoliberal ecology, this valley-landfill is just a dilemma of natural capital: a valuable land near the Rhône that serves as an experiment in decontamination and construction technologies. The geochemical and physical complexity of the site, with its mixture of air–water pollution and soil instability, has disturbed financial accounting and sparked the creativity of investors and engineers. Adding housing units and a school is the most recent solution to the riddles posed by this disobedient segment of natural capital.

As suggested in Section 1, multispecies and relational ecologies have constructed fundamental alternatives to capitalist environmentality: life does not demand management and competition but livability and cocreation. Against neoliberal imperatives, ecological quasi-subjects affirm their relational being. Their paradigm is the holobiont – "etymologically, 'entire beings' or 'safe and sound beings'" (Haraway 2016, 58) – a hybrid organic unit unthinkable as a self-contained whole. For Lynn Margulis, we are all holobionts, composite beings of heterogeneous provenance that prolong the ancestral dynamic initiated two billion years ago by the eukaryote cells, when they incorporated bacteria and archaea into their membrane and began to share their biochemical skills. From fungi and plants to animals, only the relation between hosts and other populations of symbionts such as archaea, bacteria, and viruses constitutes an ecological subjectivity, a holobiont: "All organisms large enough for us to see are composed of once-independent microbes, teamed up to become larger wholes. As they merged, many lost what we in retrospect recognize as their former individuality" (Margulis 1998, 43–4).

Without the protein coding performed by the genes of the microbiota living within us, humans would not be able to carry out their essential metabolic functions: "Estimates that 90% of the cells that comprise our bodies are bacterial belie any simple anatomical understanding of individual identity" (Gilbert, Sapp, & Tauber 2012, 327). Holobionts are a mesh of relationships, assemblages that codevelop thanks to encounters with other organisms and codetermination.

They do not recognize the separation of life and nonlife that shaped nineteenth-century biology: viruses and abiotic environmental factors are also components of their subjectivity; they determine their genome and morphology in the furnace of symbiotic exchanges (McFall-Ngai 2013). Donna Haraway has extended Margulis's notion beyond biological organisms: holobionts are "ecological assemblages" without hosts, selves, and linear derivations: "I use holobiont to mean symbiotic assemblages, at whatever scale of space or time, which are more like knots of diverse intra-active relatings in dynamic complex systems, than like the entities of a biology made up of preexisting bounded units (genes, cells, organisms, etc.) in interactions that can only be conceived as competitive or cooperative" (Haraway 2016, 60). Haraway's poetics of ecological assemblages has sparked the imagination of environmental activists, who have translated symbiotic relations into political alliances with rivers, quarries, basins, forests, and animals.[77]

Can we also imagine the "valley-waste-children-methane-degasification system" of Onex as a symbiotic being, coconstituted by contingent encounters of geomorphic forces, public health, waste disposal, and financial speculation?[78] Is this landfill-valley a strange holobiont, an assemblage of life and nonlife in which nonlife has the upper hand? Is the putrefaction of buried trash the cradle of infrastructural symbionts? I am suggesting, and excluding, this hypothesis to show why relational ecologies centered on biological phenomena cannot come to terms with the ecopolitical existence of earth-beings. The notion of the holobiont is inadequate to describe beings whose existence is dominated by subjection and unfolds in a space of nonautonomy (Hartman 1997, 61).

The third ecology instead locates the subjectivity of the Nant des Grandes-Communes in a nonbiological domain: this geobody is a restless earth-being, possessed by geochemical processes and human abuses. While persevering as a host valley, collecting waters and channeling leachates downstream, it has been filled with garbage and sprayed with DDT, covered with clay and decorated with family gardens, pierced by pipes and loaded with constructions. Builders and public authorities, owners and the local population have interacted through toxicity, engineering, and financial speculation, producing incommensurable divergences: waste strives to become methane; rainwater sustains the metabolism

---

[77] On the French Zadistes' collective personhood of "Camille-Triton," see Gosselin & gé Bartoli (2022, 87–107). Also Anna Tsing's (2015) political ethnography of matsutake mushrooms presupposes Haraway's landscape of symbiosis. The mushroom forms "polyphonic assemblages" that defeat managed plantations (Tsing 2015, 157). This mycorrhizal holobiont is an inspiring activist, a model of ecopolitical resistance against corporate attempts to standardize and enclose nature.

[78] On pervasiveness and relational materiality of waste, see Amago (2022).

of the former creek and produces leachates; landowners maximize profit; low-income citizens accept risk in exchange for affordable housing.

The Nant des Grandes-Communes is a tortured valley, a geochemical furnace, and a monument to political cynicism and methane. Its geobody has obtained its new naturalness through a process of disidentification: what used to be a small forest and a creek flowing into the Rhône is now a metabolism of methane and leachates. In a narrow sense, the Nant des Grandes-Communes could be understood as a strange holobiont: its organic components – trash, humans, and vegetable gardens – have converged in its quasi-organism. But we cannot grasp its nonautonomy if we do not refer to the principles of the third ecology. This valley-landfill exposes the contradiction between neoliberal ecologies and livability. We can attend to its political demands if we approach it as an in-between form of existence, an earth-being.

4.3 Metamorphosis

Ecological thought has rediscovered a naturalistic principle that intersects with biological imagination and Western cultural history: metamorphosis. From Ovid to Goethe and contemporary biology (Irving Williamson 2003; Ryan 2012), metamorphosis promises a life-centered worldview that glues change and continuity, morphological transformations and individual identities. Can we think of the Nant des Grandes-Communes as a metamorphosis of a valley? Is this earth-being the contemporary infrastructural manifestation of what used to be a geological formation, the metamorphic transformation of one geobody into another? Metamorphosis is a seductive principle, which explains difference by preserving the supremacy of the living.

In Ovid's *Metamorphoses*, the gods annihilate humans of the Iron Age, punishing their impiety and pride with a universal flood that submerges the Earth and the living. The only survivors, Deucalion and Pyrrha, are tasked with repopulating the world from what appears to them as a geological nature, an "empty" world "steeped in desolate silence" (Ovid 2010, 345). Desperate, they go to the Oracle of justice, Themis – the *omphalos* of Delphi – and receive this response: "Leave this temple. Veil your heads, loosen your robes, / and throw behind your back your great mother's bones" (380). Deucalion and Pyrrha interpret the Oracle's instructions, realizing that the great mother is Gaia. The lithic appearance of the world conceals a biological matrix, common stones are the bones of Gaia's living body:

> So they throw stones behind their backs which begin to grow again, transforming into human bodies: / and the stones began (who would believe it / without the testimony of antiquity?) / to lose their hardness, slowly softening / and assuming shapes. / When they had grown and taken on / a milder nature,

a certain resemblance / to human form began to be discernible, / not well
defined, but like roughed-out statues . . . / In no time at all, by divine power,
the stones / thrown by the man's hand took the form of men / and from the
woman's scattered stones women were born. (400–15)

The transition from inanimate to animate nature is described by Ovid as
a process of birth and growth, a process internal to life. Stones are bones
because Gaia is a large human body.

Ecologies attracted by the metaphysics of the person find confirmation of
the continuity of biological forms and the universality of life in the principle of
metamorphosis. For Emanuele Coccia, "all beings are the expression of one
and the same life" (Coccia 2021, 103), and therefore metamorphosis can serve
as "a theory of the continuity of life across bodies" (102). Coccia presents this
doctrine as a "multispecies and transcorporeal" rewriting of "the self and of
life" (102). Metamorphosis defuses the ecopolitical scandal of geobodies.
Thinking of the planet as a body, on the model of organic life, allows Coccia
to reinstate even atoms, rivers, and stones in biomorphic life. The Planet-
Person is the only legitimate sovereign, the great organic self, the subject that
owns life, just as the legal person owns himself and others in the legal–
political sphere: "the real subject of all metamorphoses is our planet. All
living things are nothing more than a recycling of its body" (115). Within
this biocentric metaphysics of the possession of life and the spiritual continuity of organic forms, earth-beings have no right to their own subjectivity; their
existence is brought back to the hegemony of the living: "There is no opposition between the living and the nonliving. Not only is every living creature
continuous with the nonliving, it is its extension, metamorphosis, and most
extreme expression" (5).

The site of the Nant des Grandes-Communes disproves the equivalence of
natures, which constitutes the essence of metamorphosis.[79] This valley-landfill
is not the metamorphosis of a creek but an earth-being that has lost its original
geological features. Its composite being harbors divergent natures, animated by
social exploitation and geomorphic forces: a gentle creek feeding the Rhône
River, a putrid underground landfill, some poisoned family gardens, invisible
methane emissions, dark ponds of ammonium in the woods, the design of
a modern school complex. The landfill has withdrawn from Western notions
of vital unity and organic becoming.[80] It is fragmented and lacerated, it has

---

[79] "Metamorphosis is the principle of equivalence between all natures, and the process that allows
this equivalence to arise. Every form, every nature, comes from the other and is equivalent to it.
They all exist on the same plane" (Coccia 2021, 9).

[80] On how withdrawal creates "the precondition for a radical overhaul of politics," see
Hesselberth & de Bloois (2020).

become an earth-being, subjective nonlife. In the next section, I will show how spherical sandstones in native territories of North America and river stones in Europe reproduced through artistic practices illustrate these principles of the third ecology.

5 Being the River

5.1 Sacred Stones

September 2016: the *New York Times* reporter can hardly contain his excitement sparked by the protests against the construction of the Dakota Access Pipeline (DAPL). A spontaneous political movement, combining Indigenous rights and anti-fossil fuels militancy, is born. It opposes the 1,886-kilometer-long crude oil infrastructure due to cross tribal territories and the Missouri River at the border of the Standing Rock Sioux Reservation, in North Dakota:

> Near Cannon Ball, N.D. – When visitors turn off a narrow North Dakota highway and drive into the Sacred Stone Camp, where thousands have come to protest an oil pipeline, they thread through an arcade of flags whipping in the wind. Each represents one of the 280 Native American tribes that have flocked here in what activists are calling the largest, most diverse tribal action in at least a century, perhaps since Little Bighorn. (Healy 2016)

Established by the Lakota historian and activist LaDonna Brave Bull Allard on her family land in April 2016, the Sacred Stone Camp sparked the grassroots social media movement #NoDAPL. From the spring of 2016, thousands of "water protectors" – Indigenous delegations, individual protestors, activists of Black Lives Matter, and other US and international movements – converged at Standing Rock demanding a halt to the construction of the DAPL and the destruction of sacred and burial sites.[81] The original route of the pipeline had been redirected through the reservation "in order to avoid contaminating the water of Bismarck, the capital city of North Dakota, overtly signaling that indigenous lives are inherently less valuable than white lives" (Angela Y. Davis, in Ferdinand 2022, xviii). Those at risk of contamination by oil spillages are the tribal citizens of the Standing Rock Sioux Reservation, whose farms and drinking water are now threatened by the pipeline.[82]

---

[81] See the film *Awake: A Dream from Standing Rock* (2017) (http://awakethefilm.org/).

[82] The pipeline has been rerouted by the US Army Corps of Engineers to bypass the state capital, Bismarck, because of concerns for its water supply. The pipeline is a 30-inch steel infrastructure, crossing the reservoir 100 feet below Lake Oahe, on the border of the Standing Rock Sioux Reservation. Leaks in the underground pipeline would be unfixable and undetectable for months, thus affecting the ecosystems downstream (Lakota People's Law Project 2020).

The "Sacred Stone Camp" soon became the symbol of a protest movement that inspired climate justice and Indigenous activism against fossil capitalism and land-grabbing (Proulx & Crane 2020).[83] The name of the camp is explained by Brave Bull Allard in a groundbreaking article that appeared on September 3, 2016:

> Where the Cannonball River joins the Missouri River, at the site of our camp today to stop the Dakota Access pipeline, there used to be a whirlpool that created large, spherical sandstone formations. The river's true name is *Inyan Wakangapi Wakpa*, River that Makes the Sacred Stones, and we have named the site of our resistance on my family's land the Sacred Stone Camp. The stones are not created anymore, ever since the U.S. Army Corps of Engineers dredged the mouth of the Cannonball River and flooded the area in the late 1950s as they finished the Oahe dam. They killed a portion of our sacred river. (Brave Bull Allard 2016)

The sacred stones of the Lakota are a rare geological phenomenon, spherical sandstones found in badlands of the Cannonball and the Fox Hills Formations (Figure 8).[84] *Inyan Wakangapi Wakpa* is a river inhabited by these geological singularities, which the native Lakota recognized in their storytelling as ancestral entities born in the swirling waters of the whirlpool. But European settlers saw in them only the shape of military munitions, cannonballs:

Figure 8 Cannoballs. Natural rock formations from the Cannonball River District, North Dakota, United States. Postcard, 1920s. North Dakota State University Libraries, Institute for Regional Studies.

---

[83] On fossil capital, see Malm (2016).   [84] See Biek (2015).

> LaDonna, acting as per her title of Tribal Historian, explains that when the
> expedition of Lewis and Clark arrived in 1804, "they've seen all these round
> sandstones, and the only thing they could equate them to is cannonballs. And so
> they named the Cannonball River and the community Cannonball, with com-
> plete disregard for any native name that existed prior." (Ekberzade 2018, 17)

The large sacred stones of the river have been stolen and are now driveway
ornaments of white Americans in the metropolitan area of Bismarck-Mandan.
As for the legendary whirlpool, it has been bulldozed by the US Army Corps of
Engineers, destroyed during the construction of Lake Oahe and the Oahe Dam
on the Missouri River: "In the early 1960s, as the dam neared completion, more
than 160,000 acres of the Standing Rock Sioux Reservation and 300,000 acres
of the Cheyenne River Reservation were submerged by floods resulting from its
construction" (Bengal 2018).

North Dakota's sacred stones originated about 100 million years ago during
a swift process of concretion (from the Latin *concrescere*, to grow together). These
spherical entities formed in the Cretaceous period in just a few months, a blink of an
eye in geological time: at a vertiginous growth rate, sand and silt cemented around
a nucleus of organic material, usually a shell or a plant fragment that they contain
within their stony bodies (Yoshida et al. 2018). 100 million years later, during
another crisis of presence, these geobodies once again became a singularity. At the
Sacred Stone Camp, the distinction between organic and nonorganic life collapsed,
as in those months of the Cretaceous when the spherical stones of the Cannonball
River came into existence. The water protectors gathering at the Sacred Stone Camp
have recovered the memories of Indigenous encounters with earth-beings and
translated them into political resistance to the "black snake," the oil pipeline that
has fulfilled the ancient Lakota prophecy about a black snake devastating the Earth.
While the bulldozers of Energy Transfer Partners were redrawing the geography of
land and rivers, the sacred stones pointed to an alternative world.

These geological beings resisted weathering and stood out in their environment
as totems of natural history.[85] During the #NoDAPL protests, sacred stones crossed
the lives of water protectors and reclaimed their status as earth-beings: they became
lithic protagonists of the memory of the river, political subjects. At the Sacred Stone
Camp these spherical beings have joined the fate of the native Lakota:

> We cannot forget our stories of survival. . . . On this day, 153 years ago, my
> great-great-grandmother Nape Hote Win (Mary Big Moccasin) survived the
> bloodiest conflict between the Sioux Nations and the U.S. Army ever on
> North Dakota soil. An estimated 300 to 400 of our people were killed in the

---

[85] Theodore Roosevelt National Park, Cannonball Concretions (www.nps.gov/places/cannonball-concretions.htm).

Inyan Ska (Whitestone) Massacre, far more than at Wounded Knee ... Look north and east now, toward the construction sites where they plan to drill under the Missouri River any day now, and you can see the old Sundance grounds, burial grounds, and Arikara village sites that the pipeline would destroy. Below the cliffs you can see the remnants of the place that made our sacred stones. (Brave Bull Allard 2016)

In December 2016, water protectors finally received the support of the Obama administration: the government blocked the construction of this segment of the pipeline and asked the Army Corps of Engineers to explore alternative routes. Just a few months later, in his first week in office, Donald Trump reversed the decision: since then, the pipeline has carried 470,000 barrels of crude oil per day across former Sioux land, crossing Lake Oahe and the Missouri River and endangering the water supply of the Standing Rock Sioux Reservation. Oil formed more than 300 million years ago is extracted from the Bakken formation in North Dakota and flows to the Gulf of Mexico in the metallic body of the black snake.

In March 2017, the Standing Rock Sioux Reservation, concerned about the problems caused for Cannonball residents by protesters staying at the Sacred Stone Camp, opposed Brave Bull Allard's attempt to turn the camp into a permanent eco-village and ordered its closure.[86] Brave Bull Allard died in 2021, but the legal battle against DAPL has continued to this day, with court victories by the Standing Rock Sioux Tribe, which obtained a US federal court ruling in 2020 that struck down the pipeline's permit and required a comprehensive environmental review.[87] However, the sacred stones of the Lakota have returned to their normal existence as geological curiosities and decorative cannonballs. They are still earth-beings but their ecopolitical subjectivity is latent. They are waiting for alliances to disrupt once again the perception of stones as objects and of Native Americans as disposable people. Thanks to Brave Bull Allard and the water protectors, the sacred stones have revealed their subjectivity. They reminded activists that the name Cannonball River is a colonial misnomer. The river is not carrying canno-balls. Its native denomination is *Inyan Wakangapi Wakpa*, the "River that Makes the Sacred Stones."

5.2 To Be a River

During the resistance to the construction of the DAPL and in the Māori's ancestral relationship with the Whanganui River (Section 2), humans consciously affirmed that they were one with the river, its waters, and its stones. The engagement with geobodies by the Italian sculptor Giuseppe Penone is also

---

[86] Grueskin (2017).   [87] Lakhani & agencies (2022).

premised upon a coalescence with stones and riverbeds. Penone is a protagonist of the art movement Arte Povera, which, since the late 1960s, has experimented with heterodox creative methods, found objects, and natural materials (Celant 1989).[88] In the snowy winter of 1967–8, on the sidelines of major political conflicts, Penone searched for a ground zero of artistic signification in his native Piedmontese landscape. In search of a horizontal relationship between his "person and things," he decided to "reset values" (Penone 2009, 13) by making experimental pieces with saplings, stones, and streams in a forest near Garessio, Cuneo.[89] These intimate gestures – grasping the trunk of a young tree, drawing pebbles on the river bed, lying down on the ground with his arms stretched, tying a stone to a tree with a rope or wedging stones between the branches of a tree, braiding and hugging trees, enclosing trunks in a spiral of copper wire – and the accompanying reflections and photographic documentation – have come to be recognized as a turning point in twentieth-century art (Grenier 2004). Through these actions, Penone has aligned his artistic practices with nature itself.

In *Essere fiume* (*To Be a River*, 1981–), a stone carved by a river and taken from the riverbed is placed beside another stone extracted by the artist from the mountain source of the original sample, and then sculpted to replicate it (Lancioni 2018b) (Figure 9). His aim is to be the river by acting like the river, recapitulating its actions and formative power, and producing an identical stone: "the act of sculpting does not consist in revealing a hidden aspect of nature, but in retracing the stages of natural processes and in repeating them by means of traditional sculptural techniques and materials."[90]

Penone radicalizes the aesthetic principle of *mimesis* as re-presentation. Artistic actions are a form of "tautology," a repetition of the presence of nature that removes the mediation of signs and directly applies "force and movement to elements in his environment" (Basualdo 2022, 11). Making art is to "re-present" nature, to repeat nature by imitating its forces, its material and geomorphic mechanisms. Through this tautological process, art objects are subtracted from the realm of aesthetic representation and join the subjective world of earth-beings and "magical evocation" (Interview with Penone, in Busine 2012, 11). The creative process necessary "to be a river" was described by the artist himself in 1980: "To extract a stone sculpted by the river, to travel upstream

---

[88] "Animals, plants and minerals have insurged into the art world" (Celant 2011, 118), my translation.

[89] Penone called this group of works *Alpi Marittime* (Maritime Alps) and documented them with drawings, photographs, and annotations (Celant 1989, 28-43; Lancioni 2018a).

[90] G. Penone, To Be a River, artist website (English) (https://giuseppepenone.com/en/words/to-be-a-river).

Figure 9 Giuseppe Penone, *Essere fiume* (1981). Installation view Nantes (1986). © 2023, ProLitteris, Zurich. Photo © Nanda Lanfranco.

and discover the exact point from which the stone came and extract another piece of rock from the mountain and duplicate exactly the stone taken from the river is to be the river."[91] Penone detaches a mass of stone from the mountain and works it, making it identical to the stone taken from the river, whose specific form was the result of its exposure to running water and a series of different natural accidents: rolling about, collision with other stones, and the corrosive action of the earth dragged along by the water. In the end "producing a stone of stone is perfect sculpture, it reenters nature and is cosmic heritage, a pure creation; the naturalness of the good sculpture imparts a cosmic value to it. It is being a river that is the true sculpture of stone."[92]

"Cosmic" is the term he uses to describe the plane of existence in which geobodies and humans interact as equal partners:

> Our culture has divided the ways of thinking, the human being from nature. I do not think we can make this clear distinction, there is a human matter and a matter called stone and wood, they produce cities, railways and roads, like riverbeds and mountains. From a cosmic point of view the difference between them is irrelevant. They are composed of small and big signs. They cut the forests down and there will be no oxygen, but it will be another gas, it does not change much: the oil produced through millennia is consumed and, in two–three hundred years, it will no longer exist. (Celant 1989, 19)

In *Essere fiume*, Penone applies his cosmic perspective to the river: the artist repeats the river; forces transform matter; form emerges from material encounters,

---

[91] G. Penone, To Be a River, artist website (Italian) (https://giuseppepenone.com/it/words/to-be-a-river).

[92] Ibid.

erosions, frictions. The river has taught him to deactivate Western personhood and its cult of human creativity, to put aside the separation between human subjects and natural events. The artist imagines and reproduces in his studio the exposure of the stone to the river's currents, to the random encounters with other stones.

The art historian Rémi Labrusse recalls the "overwhelming effect" on Penone of "the sight of the cave of Chauvet–Pont d'Arc" in 2012 (Labrusse 2018, 108). This Upper Paleolithic cave, the site of spectacular parietal art, disclosed to Penone another regime of artistic representation: "For me it was a real revelation in relation to the things I've seen up till now" (108). Revealed to him was "a world in which objects were no longer distinct from subjects, thanks to the extraordinary sense of having descended into the interior of a gigantic skull" (109).[93] His works are conceived as "refoundational actions" (111) that express this ontological indistinction: planetary nature itself is a "gigantic skull" (111) in which rivers and stones are subjects besides humans. The work of the artist consists in facilitating the dialogue with other-than-human subjects.

In *Essere fiume*, the original river stone has been removed from the naturalness of its place and, exhibited alongside an identical but man-made stone, it interrogates the viewer. This work exemplifies the key principle of the third ecology: earth-beings redefine the perception of nature and the scope of subjectivity. *Essere fiume* presupposes the collapse of the coordinates of Western personhood. In doing so, it also recuperates the original activity of early humans, the use of tools to modify nature. Penone's chisel remakes the river stone, bringing us back to the primal scene of the Stone Age: the material engagement of Paleolithic humans with geobodies. Revealed by the current planetary crisis, we are asked to recognize the mode of existence of a nonliving subject. *Essere fiume* is a multiplied earth-being, generated by a mountain river and then by a river-artist; a natural subject exposed to uncontrollable forces, endowed with limited agency, and occupying the cosmic dimension of human and nonhuman matter.

6 Coda

Fossil fuels are passed life, decomposed plants and organisms that over millions of years have metamorphosed into geological deposits, a subterranean realm of mineral existence that has animated the cogs of the capitalist world-ecology for over 100 years. Deeply rooted in its colonial matrix, fossil capitalism has destabilized planetary life. The billions of tons of fossil fuels extracted and

---

[93] For a critique of the Neolithic/Paleolithic imaginary in contemporary environmental discourse, see Pedriali (2021).

burned, the savage urbanization of entire continents, and the intensification of monocultures have left immense scars on the Earth, altered the composition of the atmosphere, and compromised ocean circulation. In this Element, I borrowed from Ernesto De Martino the expression "crisis of presence" to reflect on the erosion of the boundaries that separate the human condition from the terrestrial condition. At the current juncture of natural and social history, in our post-Holocenic age of climate meltdown, regimes of extraction and pollution have reshaped and established notions of personhood: other-than-human subjects – plants, animals, bacteria, symbionts, abiotic entities – demand recognition alongside humans; they inhabit the Earth with us. Beyond neoliberal ecologies that optimize the reproduction of natural capital, and multispecies approaches that map the fluidity and continuum of life, I advocated the urgency of a third ecology, one that gives voice to nonliving subjects – earth-beings.

Geobodies encourage us to disassemble Western personhood and relativize biocentrism. From rocks and rivers we can learn what earthly subjects do and what they look like, when all-too-human preoccupations do not blind the gaze. Earth-beings are not swayed by desires and cognitions but they are affected, they move or stand still, they linger, pollute, or weather away, experiencing the forces of the Earth as variations of their existence. Their presence sidesteps biological life, their vicissitudes unravel along organisms of which they witness the survival and extinction. The third ecology is a disciple of naturalistic thought, art practices, philosophies, religions, and social movements that have redesigned the perception of the world from the perspective of geobodies: Japanese Shinto rituals, Andean *tirakuna*, Deleuzian "bodies without organs," pluriversal, ecofeminist, and multispecies ecopolitics.

In the Western pantheon of the third ecology, a prominent space is occupied by Baruch Spinoza, the Dutch Golden Age philosopher who dissolved God into nature, using the example of a stone to mock human personhood and its free will. Three centuries before Italo Calvino gave voice to a stone to reveal the gap that separates the Western human *persona* from natural subjects, Spinoza, in a 1674 letter, invited his friend Georg Hermann Schuller to imagine a stone that thinks "as it moves":

> But let's examine created things, which are all determined by external causes to exist and to produce effects in a definite and determinate way. To clearly understand this, let's conceive something very simple. Suppose a stone receives, from an external cause which strikes against it, a certain quantity of motion, by which it afterward will necessarily continue to move, even though the impulse of the external cause ceases. This continuance of the stone in motion, then, is compelled, not because it is necessary, but because it must be defined by the impulse of the external cause. What I say here about the

stone must be understood concerning any singular thing, however composite it is conceived to be, and however capable of doing many things: each thing is necessarily determined by some external cause to exist and produce effects in a certain and determinate way. Next, conceive now, if you will, that while the stone continues to move, it thinks, and knows that as far as it can, it strives to continue moving. Of course, since the stone is conscious only of its striving, and not at all indifferent, it will believe that it is very free, and that it perseveres in motion for no other cause than because it wills to. This is that famous human freedom everyone brags of having, which consists only in this: that men are conscious of their appetite and ignorant of the causes by which they are determined. (Spinoza 2016, 428)

If only this stone could think, Spinoza argues, it would repeat the same misunderstandings that haunt humans: it would detach its ways of being (its "effort") from the forces of nature; it would mistake external causes for its will, and its movement for its freedom; and it would believe that consciousness places it above all beings. Spinoza suggests instead that stones are wiser than humans: thanks to their lithic nonlife and blissful naivety, they move but do not think. By observing a common stone, its subjective and nonhuman being, we realize that "the famous human freedom everyone brags of having" does not exist in nature, and it does not make humans autonomous persons. Moreover, the lack of consciousness, a paramount feature of earth-beings, is praised indirectly by Spinoza as a superior quality: since they do not think, stones do not justify their deeds and "appetite" through deceitful notions. The relational field in which geobodies are immersed demystifies human consciousness and points to a more inclusive notion of subjectivity.

Earth-beings bear the traces of the transitional events during which they came into existence: erratics cannot disguise their Ice Age origin in glacial retreats; *inqaychus*, the small stone animals of the Andes, emerge from cosmic and historical ruptures; the sacred stones of Standing Rock originated as geological odds in the Cretacious period and became symbols of autonomy and resistance during the No-DAPL protests. These geobodies took shape in times of crisis, conjunctures that produced singular inhabitants. The present environmental crisis is making us aware again of this common denominator of the terrestrial condition: in the planetary drama of life and nonlife, we are subjects just as stones and rivers, animals and plants are subjects. Together, we are exposed to turmoil and catastrophes, removed by climate change and terricides "from the naturalness of a place" (Rancière 1999, 36) and molded into new subjects by unrestrained forces of disidentification. This ecopolitical predicament is not an exception in the saga of the universe: it reiterates on a planetary scale the cosmic origin of the heavy elements, the cataclysms that formed the materials of which all earth-beings and living organisms are made.

The universe's hydrogen, helium, and lithium were produced 13.8 billion years ago within the first three minutes of the Big Bang. The origin of elements in the periodic table up to the atomic mass of iron is different: they are made "in the hot cores of short-lived massive stars. There, nuclear fusion creates ever-heavier elements as it powers the star and causes it to shine" (Frebel & Beers 2018, 30). Astrophysicists have discovered in recent decades that elements heavier than iron came instead from slow processes of neutron-capture that occurred in the late stages of the evolution of massive stars, and in incredibly rapid and violent events: explosions of supernova stars and the fusion of binary neutron stars. In particular, collisions of neutron stars happening all across the universe were the forges of heavy elements. Most of the gold, silver, platinum, and uranium, as well as other heavy chemical elements on Earth, were formed in a fraction of a second during these unimaginable catastrophes. No other cosmic event, with exception of the merging of black holes, involves comparable amounts of energy and transform-ation of matter, space, and time. In August 2017, the theoretical models of nuclear physicists found a stunning empirical confirmation when the LIGO and VIRGO gravitational wave detectors in the United States and Italy recorded a ripple in space–time in a galaxy 130 million light-years from Earth (Burtnyk 2017). Two neutron stars revolving around each other had ended their lives, collapsing into a single object, releasing an immense amount of energy, called a "kilonova." This event took place when dinosaurs were still roaming the Earth but the electromag-netic waves and the deformation of space–time caused by the kilonova reached our planet only in 2017.

What happened in this corner of the universe? Researchers have observed the fusion of two neutron stars, the densest objects in the cosmos, which have a radius of about 12 kilometers and a mass 1.2–1.5 times that of our sun. These celestial bodies are corpses of large dead stars, cosmic beings in which a spoon of matter would weigh more than the largest mountain on Earth. When a pair of such astronomical ghosts are bound in a binary system, instead of slowly cooling off, they can end their lives by spiraling into an explosive collision, sending across the universe gravitational waves, radioactive debris, and a short gamma-ray burst. Using the LIGO and VIRGO gravitational wave detectors, astronomers have captured one of these cataclysms of space–time and found in its electromagnetic spectrum evidence of the instantaneous formation of immense masses of gold, platinum, uranium, and other elements that can seed an entire galaxy (Curtis 2023).

We can now understand Penone's cosmic point of view: we share with earth-beings a stellar origin, we are the terrestrial leftovers of these forces, the result of the most intense events in the universe. Geobodies are before all life and above all life. They are the purest mode of existence of an unconstructable material reality that no human technology will be able to recreate, producing on Earth the incommensurable conditions of heat, density, and pressure of the elements' cataclysmic birthplace. Suspended between this ancient beginning and their vulnerable existence in the capitalist world-ecology, earth-beings are now humble material witnesses of the blindest actions of biological life: humans' destruction of the planet.

References

Aboriginal Areas Protection Authority (AAPA) (2013). Bootu Creek Court Case – Historic Conviction of Miner for Desecrating Sacred Site, August 2, www.aapant.org.au/system/files/fileuploads/bootu_creek_media_release_2_august_2013_1.pdf.

Agassiz, L. (2012). *Études Sur Les Glaciers*. Cambridge: Cambridge University Press.

Allen, C. J. (1988). *The Hold Life Has: Coca and Cultural Identity in an Andean Community*. Washington: Smithsonian Institution Press.

  (2015). The Whole World Is Watching: New Perspectives on Andean Animism. In T. L. Bray, ed., *The Archaeology of Wak'as: Explorations of the Sacred in the Pre-Columbian Andes*. Boulder: University Press of Colorado.

  (2016a). Stones Who Love Me: Dimensionality, Enclosure and Petrification in Andean Culture. *Archives de sciences sociales des religions*, 174, 327–46.

  (2016b). The Living Ones: Miniatures and Animation in the Andes. *Journal of Anthropological Research*, 72(4), 416–41.

Alloa, E. & Larison, L. (2020). Entretien avec Philippe Descola. *Cités*, 81, 23–43.

Amago, S. (2022). *Basura: Cultures of Waste in Contemporary Spain*. Charlottesville: University of Virginia Press.

Anker, P. (2001). *Imperial Ecology: Environmental Order in the British Empire, 1895–1945*. Cambridge, MA: Harvard University Press.

Ansell-Pearson, K. (1997). *Viroid Life: Perspectives on Nietzsche and the Transhuman Condition*. London: Routledge.

Ari, W. (2014). *Earth Politics: Religion, Decolonization, and Bolivia's Indigenous Intellectuals*. Durham, NC: Duke University Press.

Armiero, M. (2021). *Wasteocene: Stories from the Global Dump*. Cambridge: Cambridge University Press.

Arneil, B. (1996). *John Locke and America: The Defence of English Colonialism*. Oxford: Oxford University Press.

Aronoff, K., Battistoni, A., Aldana Cohen, D., Riofrancos, T. N., & Klein, N. (2019). *A Planet to Win: Why We Need a Green New Deal*. London: Verso.

Bakker, K. (2015). Neoliberalization of Nature. In T. Perreault, G. Bridge, & J. Mc Carthy, eds., *The Routledge Handbook of Political Ecology*. London: Routledge.

Baltrusaitis, J. (1957). *Aberrations*. Paris: Perrin.

Barca, S. (2020). *Forces of Reproduction: Notes for a Counter-Hegemonic Anthropocene*. Cambridge: Cambridge University Press.

Basualdo, C., ed. (2022). *Rivers of Forms: Giuseppe Penone's Drawings*. Philadelphia, PA: Philadelphia Museum of Art.

Bengal, R. (2018). What Lies Beneath Lake Oahe: Looking at the Past from the Shores of Standing Rock. *Lapham's Quarterly*, July 11, www.laphamsquar terly.org/roundtable/what-lies-beneath-lake-oahe.

Bennett, J. (2009). *Vibrant Matter: A Political Ecology of Things*. Durham, NC: Duke University Press.

Bernard, R., Reynard, E., & Jacob, A. (2013). Histoire de la Pierre des Marmettes et rôle de La Murithienne. *Bulletin de la Murithienne*, 130, 13–17.

Biek, B. (2015). Concretions and Nodules in North Dakota, www.dmr.nd.gov/ndgs/ndnotes/concretions/concretions.asp.

Blaser, M. (2013). Notes toward a Political Ontology of Environmental Conflicts. In L Green, ed., *Contested Ecologies: Dialogues in the South on Nature and Knowledge*. Cape Town: Human Sciences Research Council Press.

Bobbette, A. & Donovan, A., eds. (2019). *Political Geology: Active Stratigraphies and the Making of Life*. Cham: Palgrave.

Bonneuil, C. (2020). Der Historiker und der Planet: Planetaritatsregimes an der Schnittstelle von Welt-Okologien, ökologischen Reflexivitaten und Geo-Machten. In F. Adloff and S. Neckel, eds., *Gesellschaftstheorie im Anthropozän*. Frankfurt: Campus.

Bonneuil, C. & Fressoz, J. B. (2016). *The Shock of the Anthropocene: The Earth, History, and Us*. New York: Verso.

Bourgeois-Gironde, S. (2020). *Être la rivière* (illustrated edition). Paris: PUF.

Brave Bull Allard, L. (2016). Why the Founder of Standing Rock Sioux Camp Can't Forget the Whitestone Massacre. *Yes! Solutions Journalism*, September 3, www.yesmagazine.org/democracy/2016/09/03/why-the-founder-of-standing-rock-sioux-camp-cant-forget-the-whitestone-massacre.

Bray, T. L., ed. (2015). *The Archaeology of Wak'as: Explorations of the Sacred in the Pre-Columbian Andes*. Boulder: University Press of Colorado.

Burgio, V. & Guaraldo, E. (2022). Ice Core Verticality: the Eloquence of Ice and the Visual Construction of Deep Time. *Elephant & Castle*, 28(2), 56–68.

Burtnyk, K. (2017). LIGO Detection of Colliding Neutron Stars Spawns Global Effort to Study the Rare Event, *LIGO Laboratory*, October 16, www.ligo.caltech.edu/news/ligo20171016.

Busine, L., ed. (2012). *Giuseppe Penone*. Milan: Electa.

Caillois, R. (1985). *The Writing of Stones*. Charlottesville: University of Virginia Press.

Calvino, I. (2005). *Romanzi e racconti*. Vol. 3. Milan: Mondadori.

Calzadilla, V. & Kotzé, L. (2018). Living in Harmony with Nature? A Critical Appraisal of the Rights of Mother Earth in Bolivia. *Transnational Environmental Law*, 7(3), 397–424.

Canguilhem, G. (2008). *Knowledge of life*. New York: Fordham University Press.

Castree, N. (2008). Neoliberalising Nature: The Logics of Deregulation and Reregulation. *Environment and Planning A: Economy and Space*, 40(1), 131–52.

Celant, G. (1989). *Giuseppe Penone*. Milan: Electa.

  (2011). *Arte povera: Storia e storie*. Milan: Electa.

Cesaretti, E. (2020). *Elemental Narratives: Reading Environmental Entanglements in Modern Italy*. University Park: Penn State University Press

Chakrabarty, D. (2009). The Climate of History: Four Theses. *Critical Inquiry*, 35(2), 197–222.

Charpentier, J. de. (1841). *Essai sur les glaciers et sur le terrain erratique du bassin du Rhône*. Lausanne: M. Ducloux.

Chase, Z. J. (2015). What Is a Wak'a? When Is a Wak'a? In T. L. Bray, ed., *The Archaeology of Wak'as: Explorations of the Sacred in the Pre-Columbian Andes*. Boulder: University Press of Colorado.

Ciplet, D. & Timmons Roberts, J. (2017). Climate Change and the Transition to Neoliberal Environmental Governance. *Global Environmental Change*, 46, 148–56.

Clark, N. & Yusoff, K. (2017). Geosocial Formations and the Anthropocene. *Theory, Culture & Society*, 34(2–3), 3–23.

Clarke, A. C. (1968). *2001: A Space Odyssey*. New York: New American Library.

Clarke, B. (2017). Rethinking Gaia: Stengers, Latour, Margulis. *Theory, Culture & Society*, 34(4), 3–26.

Clayton, S. (2020). Climate anxiety: Psychological Responses to Climate Change. *Journal of Anxiety Disorders*, 74(102263), 1–7, https://doi.org/10.1016/j.janxdis.2020.102263.

Coccia, E. (2021). *Metamorphoses*. Cambridge: Polity Press.

Coglitore, R. (2004). *Pietre figurate. Forme del fantastico e mondo minerale*. Pisa: ETS.

Cohen, J. J. (2015). *Stone: An Ecology of the Inhuman*. Minneapolis: University of Minnesota Press.

Colebrook, C. (2014). *Essays on Extinction: Death of the Posthuman*. London: Open Humanities Press.

Conseil Municipal de Genève (2003). PR-203A (159e): Frais d'assainissement de l'ancienne décharge du Nant des Grandes-Communes, https://bit.ly/3rg5MV3.

Crosby, A. (2004). *Ecological Imperialism: The Biological Expansion of Europe, 900–1900*. Cambridge: Cambridge University Press.

Crutzen, P. (2002). Geology of Mankind. *Nature*, 23(415), 23.

Curley, M. J., trans. (1979). *Physiologus*. Chicago, IL: University of Chicago Press.

Curtis, S. (2023). Cosmic Alchemy. *Scientific American*, 328(1), 30–7.

D'Avignon, R. (2020). Spirited Geobodies: Producing Subterranean Property in Nineteenth-Century Bambuk, West Africa. *Technology and Culture*, 61(2), 20–48.

Dardot, P. & Laval, C. (2014). *The New Way of the World: On Neoliberal Society*. New York: Verso.

Davidson, J. (1995). Zeus and the Stone Substitute. *Hermes*, 123(3), 363–9.

Dean, C. J. (2010). *A Culture of Stone: Inka Perspectives on Rock*. Durham: Duke University Press.

Debaise, D. (2008). The Dynamics of Possession. In D Skribna, ed., *Mind that Abides. Panpsychism in the new millenium*. Amsterdam: John Benjamins.

   (2017a). *Nature as Event. The Lure of the Possible*. Durham: Duke University Press

   (2017b). Les puissances subjectives de la nature selon Gabriel Tarde. *Cahiers de philosophie de l'université de Caen*, 54, 135–46, https://journals.open edition.org/cpuc/325.

de la Cadena, M. (2015). *Earth Beings: Ecologies of Practice across Andean Worlds*. Durham, NC: Duke University Press.

   (2023). Stengers Meets an Andean Mountain That Is Not Only Such. In N. Bubandt & T. Schwarz Wentzer, eds., *Philosophy of Fieldwork: Case Studies in Anthropological Analysis*. London: Routledge.

de la Cadena, M. & Blaser, M. (2018). *A World of Many Worlds*. Durham, NC: Duke University Press.

De Martino, E. (2015). *Magic: A Theory from the South*. London: Hau Books.

Dean, C. J. (2010). *A Culture of Stone: Inka Perspectives on Rock*. Durham, NC: Duke University Press.

Debaise, D. (2008). The Dynamics of Possession. In D Skribna, ed., *Mind That Abides: Panpsychism in the New Millenium*. Amsterdam: John Benjamins.

(2017a). *Nature as Event: The Lure of the Possible*. Durham, NC: Duke University Press

(2017b). Les puissances subjectives de la nature selon Gabriel Tarde. *Cahiers de philosophie*

Dehm, J. (2018). One Tonne of Carbon Dioxide Equivalent (1tCO2e). In J. Hohmann & D. Joyce, eds., *International Law's Objects*. Oxford: Oxford University Press.

Deleuze, G. (1993). *The Fold: Leibniz and the Baroque*. London: The Athlone Press.

Deleuze, G. & Guattari, F. (1987). *A Thousand Plateaus*, translated by Brian Massumi. Minneapolis: University of Minnesota Press.

Descola, P. (2005). *Beyond Nature and Culture*. Chicago, IL: The University of Chicago Press.

Directorate-General for Communication of the European Commission (DG COMM) (2022). Delivering the European Green Deal, https://commis sion.europa.eu/strategy-and-policy/priorities-2019-2024/european-green-deal_en.

Donaldson, S. & Kymlicka, W. (2011). *Zoopolis: A Political Theory of Animal Rights*. Oxford: Oxford University Press.

Dreyfus, H. L. & Rabinow, P. (2014). *Michel Foucault: Beyond Structuralism and Hermeneutics*. Chicago, IL: The University of Chicago Press.

Ejército Zapatista de Liberación Nacional (1996). Cuarta Declaración de la Selva Lacandona, January 1.

Ekberzade, B. (2018). *Standing Rock: Greed, Oil and the Lakota's Struggle for Justice*. London: ZED.

Escobar, A. (2018). *Designs for the Pluriverse*. Durham, NC: Duke University Press.

Escobar, A., Osterweil, M., & Sharma, K. (2022). *Pluriversal Horizons: Notes for an Onto-Epistemic Reorientation of Technology*. In A. Majaca, ed., *Incomputable Earth: Digital Technologies and the Anthropocene*. London: Bloomsbury.

Esposito, R. (2012a). *Third Person: Politics of Life and Philosophy of the Impersonal*. Oxford: Polity.

(2012b). The Dispositif of the Person. *Law, Culture and The* Humanities, 8(1), 17–30.

(2015). *Persons and Things: From the Body's Point of View*. London: John Wiley & Sons.

Farrier, D. (2019). *Anthropocene Poetics: Deep Time, Sacrifice Zones, and Extinctions*. Minneapolis: The University of Minnesota Press

Favre, A. & Studer, B. (1867). *Appel aux Suisses pour les encourager à conserver les blocs erratiques*. Rheinfelden: Actes de la Société helvétique des sciences naturelles.

Federici, S. (2004). *Caliban and the Witch*. New York: Autonomedia.

Ferdinand, M. (2022). *Decolonial Ecology: Thinking from the Caribbean World*. Oxford: Polity.

Frebel, A. & Beers, T. C. (2018). The formation of the heaviest elements. *Physics Today*, 71(1), 30–7.

Galindo, R. J. (2017). Desierto-Piedra [Desert-Stone]. *Ecozon@*, 8(1), 195–201.

Galindo, R. J. & Murphy Turner, M. (2021). On the Violence of the World: A Conversation with Regina José Galindo, *MoMA*, January 12, www.moma.org/magazine/articles/484.

García Linera, Á. (2012). *Geopolítica de la Amazonía: Poder hacendal patrimonial y acumulación capitalista*. La Paz: Vicepresidencia del Estado, Presidencia de la Asamblea Legislativa Plurinacional.

Gentili, D. (2021). *The Age of Precarity: Endless Crisis as an Art of Government*. New York: Verso Books.

Gibson, J. (2015). *The Ecological Approach to Visual Perception*. New York: Taylor & Francis.

Gilbert, S. F., Sapp J., & Tauber A. (2012). A Symbiotic View of Life: We Have Never Been Individuals. *Quarterly Review of Biology*, 87(4), 325–41.

Girardclos, S. (2019). Living and Working on a Waste Landfill: A Post-War Boom Legacy in Geneva. In *Workshop Beyond Recycling: Crossed Perspectives on the Management of Waste, Remains and Surplus*. Geneva, February 5, https://archive-ouverte.unige.ch/unige:142020.

Goethe, J. W. von (2016). *The Essential Goethe*, edited by M. Bell. Princeton, NJ: Princeton University Press.

Gómez-Barris, M. (2017). *The Extractive Zone: Social Ecologies and Decolonial Perspectives*. Durham, NC: Duke University Press.

Górska-Zabielska, M. (2021). The Rock Garden of the Institute of Geography and Environmental Sciences, Jan Kochanowski University – A New Geo-Site in Kielce, Central Poland. *Geosciences*, 11(3), 113, www.mdpi.com/2076-3263/11/3/113.

Gosselin, S. & gé Bartoli, D. (2022). *La condition terrestre: Habiter la Terre en communs*. Paris: Seuil.

Goto, K., Kawana, T., & Imamura, F. (2010). Historical and Geological Evidence of Boulders Deposited by Tsunamis, Southern Ryukyu Islands, Japan. *Earth-Science Reviews*, 102(1), 77–99.

Grenier, C. (2004). *Giuseppe Penone*. Paris: Centre Pompidou.

Grove, R. H. (1997). *Ecology, Climate and Empire: Colonialism and Global Environmental History, 1400–1940*. London: White Horse Press.

Grueskin, G. (2017). Sacred Stone Camp Closed, Protesters Leave. *Bismarck Tribune*, March 1, https://bit.ly/463qdDL.

Haraway, D. H. (2016). *Staying with the Trouble: Making Kin in the Chthulucene*. Durham, NC: Duke University Press.

Hartman, Sanidiya V. (1997). *Scenes of Subjection: Terror, Slavery, and Self-making in Nineteenth-Century America*. Oxford: Oxford University Press.

Harvey, D. (2007). Neoliberalism as Creative Destruction. *Annals of the American Academy of Political and Social Science*, 610, 22–44.

Hattori, H., Shitamichi, M., Yasuno, T., Ishikura, T., & Nousaku, F. (2019). *Cosmo-Eggs*. Tokyo: Case Publishing.

Hayek, F. A. von. (2012). *Law, Legislation and Liberty*. London: Routledge.

Healy, J. (2016). From 280 Tribes, a Protest on the Plains. *New York Times*, Sept. 11, www.nytimes.com/interactive/2016/09/12/us/12tribes.html?searchResultPosition=9.

Hecht, S. B. (2013). *Preface*. In D. Hindery, ed., *From Enron to Evo: Pipeline Politics, Global Environmentalism, and Indigenous Rights in Bolivia*. Tucson: University of Arizona Press.

Hesiod (2006). *Hesiod: Theogony and Works and Days*, translated by Catherine Schlegel and Henry Weinfield. Ann Arbor: University of Michigan Press.

Hesselberth, P. & de Bloois, J., eds. (2020). *Politics of Withdrawal: Media, Arts, Theory*. London: Rowman & Littlefield

Heynen, N. (2007). *Neoliberal Environments: False Promises and Unnatural Consequences*. London: Routledge.

Höhler, S. (2015). *Spaceship Earth in the Environmental Age, 1960–1990*. London: Routledge.

Hopes, A. & Perry, L. (2019). *Reflections on the Plantationocene: A conversation with Donna Haraway and Anna Tsing*, moderated by Gregg Mitman. *Edge Effects Magazine*, Nelson Institute, University of Wisconsin–Madison.

Hui, Y. (2019). *Recursivity and Contingency*. London: Rowman & Littlefield.

Hustak, C. & Myers, N. (2012). Involutionary Momentum: Affective Ecologies and the Sciences of Plant/Insect Encounters. *Differences*, 23(3), 74–118.

Hutton, J. M. (2013). Erratic Imaginaries: Thinking Landscape as Evidence. In E. Turpin, ed., *Architecture in the Anthropocene: Encounters among Design, Deep Time, Science and Philosophy*. London: Open Humanities Press.

Ingold, T. (2000). *The Perception of the Environment: Essays on Livelihood, Dwelling and Skill*. Hove: Psychology Press.

(2013). *Making: Anthropology, Archaeology, Art and Architecture*. London: Routledge.

(2016). A Naturalist Abroad in the Museum of Ontology: Philippe Descola's *Beyond Nature and Culture*. *Anthropological Forum*, 26(3), 301–20.

Iovino, S. (2014). Bodies of Naples: Stories, Matter, and the Landscapes of Porosity. In S. Iovino & S. Oppermann, eds., *Material Ecocriticism*. Bloomington: Indiana University Press.

(2017). Editorial: Creative Writing and Art: South Atlantic Ecocriticism. *Ecozon@*, 8(1), 189–94.

(2019). *The Reverse of the Sublime: Dilemmas (and Resources) of the Anthropocene Garden*. Munich: Rachel Carson Center Perspectives.

Iovino, S. & Oppermann, S. (2014). *Material Ecocriticism*. Bloomington: Indiana University Press.

Irving Williamson, D. (2003). *The Origins of Larvae*. Dordrecht: Springer Science+Business Media.

Jabr, F. (2020). The Social Life of Forests. *New York Times*, December 6, www.nytimes.com/interactive/2020/12/02/magazine/tree-communica tion-mycorrhiza.html.

Jan-Hess, I. (2016). Onex: Des tours et une nouvelle école aux Tattes. *Tribune de Genève*, April 21.

Janusek, J. W. (2012). Understanding Tiwanaku Origins: Animistic Ecology in the Andean Altiplano. In C. Isendahl, ed., *The Past Ahead: Language, Culture, and Identity in the Neotropics*. Uppsala: Uppsala University.

Kirksey, E. & Helmreich, S. (2010). The Emergence of Multispecies Ethnography. *Cultural Anthropology*, 25(4), 545–76.

Kirksey, E., Schuetze, C., & Helmreich, S. (2014) *The Multispecies Salon*. Durham, NC: Duke University Press.

Kohn, E. (2013). *How Forests Think: Toward an Anthropology beyond the Human*. Berkeley: University of California Press.

Kothari, A., Salleh, A., Escobar, A., Demaria, F., & Acosta, A. (2019). *Pluriverse: A Post-Development Dictionary*. New Delhi: Tulika.

La Follette, C., & Maser, C. (2019). *Sustainability and the Rights of Nature: An Introduction*. London: Routledge.

Labrusse, R. (2018). The End of the Neolithic. In C. Basualdo, ed., *The Inner Life of Forms*. New York: Rizzoli International Publications.

Lakhani, N. & agencies (2022). US Supreme Court Rejects Dakota Access Pipeline Appeal. *Guardian*, February 22, www.theguardian.com/us-news/ 2022/feb/22/us-supreme-court-dakota-access-pipeline.

Lakota People's Law Project (2020). DAPL's Dangerous Leak Detection System, https://lakotalaw.org/news/2020-07-17/dapl-leak-detection.

Lancioni, D. (2018a). I: Alpi Marittime [Maritime Alps]. In Basualdo, C. ed., *The Inner Life of Forms*. New York: Rizzoli International Publications.

(2018b). VI: Essere fiume [To Be a River]. In Basualdo, C. ed., *The Inner Life of Forms*. New York: Rizzoli International Publications.

Landivar, D. & Ramillien, E. (2017). Savoirs autochtones, "nature-sujet" et gouvernance environnementale: Une analyse des reconfigurations du droit et de la politique en Bolivie et en Équateur. *Autrepart*, 81(1), 135–58.

Latour, B. (1999). *Politics of Nature: How to Bring the Sciences into Democracy*. Cambridge, MA: Harvard University Press.

(2017). *Facing Gaia: Eight Lectures on the New Climatic Regime*. Oxford: Polity.

Lele, S., Springate-Baginski, O., Lakerveld, R., Deb, D., & Dash, P. (2013). Ecosystem Services: Origins, Contributions, Pitfalls, and Alternatives. *Conservation and Society*, 11(4), 343–58.

Leopardi, G. (1997). *Zibaldone*. Milan: Newton Compton.

Lerner, S. (2012). *Sacrifice Zones: The Front Lines of Toxic Chemical Exposure in the United States*. Cambridge: MIT Press.

Lewis, S. L., & Maslin, M. A. (2015). Defining the Anthropocene. *Nature*, 519, 171–80.

Lindgaard, J., ed. (2018). *Éloge des mauvaises herbes, ce que nous devons à la ZAD*. Paris: Les liens qui libèrent.

Lohmann, L. (2016). Neoliberalism's Climate. In S. Springer, K. Birch, & J. MacLeavy, eds., *Handbook of Neoliberalism*. London: Routledge.

Lovelock, J. (1979). *Gaia, a New Look at Life on Earth*. Oxford: Oxford University Press.

Lovelock, J. & Margulis, L. (1974). Atmospheric Homeostasis by and for the Biosphere: The Gaia Hypothesis. *Tellus*, 26(1–2), 2–10.

Lugones, M. (2010). Towards a Decolonial Feminism. *Hypatia*, 25(4), 742–59.

Luisetti, F. (2019). Geopower: On the States of Nature of Late Capitalism. *European Journal of Social Theory*, 22(3), 342–63.

(2021). L'ecologia politica di Giacomo Leopardi. *Rivista Internazionale di Studi Leopardiani*, 13, 149–61.

(2022). The Neoliberal Virus. In V. Lemm & M. Vatter, eds., *The Viral Politics of Covid-19: Nature, Home, and Planetary Health*. Singapore: Springer Nature.

Macrì, S. (2009). *Pietre viventi. I minerali nell'immaginario del mondo antico*. Turin: UTET.

Malafouris, L. (2013). *How Things Shape the Mind: A Theory of Material Engagement*. Cambridge: MIT Press.

Malm, A. (2016). *Fossil Capital: The Rise of Steam Power and the Roots of Global Warming*. New York: Verso.

Maloney, M. & Burdon, P., eds. (2014). *Wild Law – In Practice*. London: Taylor & Francis.

Mancuso, S. (2021). *The Nation of Plants*. New York: Other Press.

Mannheim, B. & Salas Carreño, G. (2015). Wak'as: Entifications of the Andean Sacred. In T. L. Bray, ed., *The Archaeology of Wak'as: Explorations of the Sacred in the Pre-Columbian Andes*. Boulder: University of Colorado Press.

Maran, T. (2014). Semiotization of Matter: A Hybrid Zone between Biosemiotics and Material Ecocriticism. In S. Iovino & S. Oppermann, eds., *Material Ecocriticism*. Bloomington: Indiana University Press.

(2020). *Ecosemiotics*. Cambridge: Cambridge University Press.

Margulis, L. (1991). Symbiogenesis and Symbionticism. In L. Margulis & R. Fester, eds., *Symbiosis as a Source of Evolutionary Innovation: Speciation and Morphogenesis*. Cambridge: MIT Press.

(1998). *Symbiotic Planet: A New Look at Evolution*. New York: Basic Books.

Martinez-Alier, J. (2002). *The Environmentalism of the Poor: A Study of Ecological Conflicts and Valuation*. Northhampton, MA: Edward Elgar Publishing.

(2010). Social Metabolism, Ecological Distribution Conflicts, and Valuation Languages. *Capitalism Nature Socialism*, 20(1), 58–87.

Masco, J. (2014). *The Theater of Operations: National Security Affect from the Cold War to the War on Terror*. Durham, NC: Duke University Press.

Massey, D. (2005). *For Space*. New York: SAGE Publications.

Mauss, M. (1985). A Category of the Human Mind: The Notion of Person; the Notion of Self. In M. Carrithers, S. Collins, & S. Lukes, eds., *The Category of the Person: Anthropology, Philosophy, History*. Cambridge: Cambridge University Press.

Mbembe, A. (2019). *Necropolitics*. Durham, NC: Duke University Press.

McFall-Ngai, M., Hadfield, M., Bosch T., et al. (2013). Animals in a Bacterial World: A New Imperative for the Life Sciences. *Proceedings of the National Academy of Sciences*, 110(9), 3229–36.

Mendoza, M. (2021). El Movimiento de Mujeres Indígenas por el Buen Vivir: Intersticios de una lucha feminista, antiextractivista y por la Plurinacionalidad. *Cuadernos del Centro de Estudios en Diseño y Comunicación. Ensayos*, 91, 109–29.

Mezzadra, S., & Neilson, B. (2019). *The Politics of Operations: Excavating Contemporary Capitalism*. Durham, NC: Duke University Press.

Mignolo, W. D. (2002). The Geopolitics of Knowledge and the Colonial Difference. *South Atlantic Quarterly*, 101(1), 57–96.

(2021). *The Politics of Decolonial Investigations: On Decoloniality.* Durham, NC: Duke University Press.

Mirowski, P. & Plehwe, D. (2009). *The Road from Mont Pèlerin: The Making of the Neoliberal Thought Collective.* Cambridge, MA: Harvard University Press.

Moore, J. W. (2000). Sugar and the Expansion of the Early Modern World-Economy: Commodity Frontiers, Ecological Transformation, and Industrialization. *Review (Fernand Braudel Center)*, 23(3), 409–33.

(2016). *Anthropocene or Capitalocene? Nature, History, and the Crisis of Capitalism.* Oakland, CA: PM Press.

Morton, T. (2013). *Philosophy and Ecology After the End of the World.* Minneapolis: University of Minnesota Press.

Motta, M. (2007). *Erratic Blocks: From Protector Beings to Geosites to Be Protected.* In L. Piccardi & W. B. Masse, eds., *Myth and Geology.* London: Geological Society, Special Publications.

Murúa, Martín de (2004 [1590]). *Historia de los Incas: Historia y genealogía de los reyes Incas del Perú. Códice Galvin*, Juan Ossio, ed. Madrid: Testimonio Compañía Editorial.

Mussawir, E. & Parsley, C. (2017). The Law of Persons Today: At the Margins of Jurisprudence. *Law and Humanities*, 11(1), 44–63.

Mussgnug, F. (2019). Species at War? The Animal and the Anthropocene. *Paragraph*, 42(1), 116–30.

Neimanis, A. & Loewen Walker, R. (2014). Weathering: Climate Change and the "Thick Time" of Transcorporeality. *Hypatia*, 29(3), 558–75.

Nixon, R. (2022). The Less Selfish Gene: Forest Altruism, Neoliberalism, and the Tree of Life. Stockholm Archipelago Lecture, November 10, www.kth.se/blogs/hist/2022/10/upcoming-rob-nixon-at-the-11th-stockholm-archipelago-lecture/.

O'Donnell, E. (2018). *Legal Rights for Rivers: Competition, Collaboration and Water Governance.* London: Routledge.

Odum, H. T. & Odum, E. C. (2000). *Modeling for all Scales: An introduction to System Simulation.* San Diego, CA: Academic Press

Ovid (2010). *Metamorphoses*, translated by S. Lombardo. Indianapolis, IN: Hackett Publishing Company.

Parr, A. (2014). *The Wrath of Capital: Neoliberalism and Climate Change Politics.* New York. Columbia University Press.

Pedriali, F. (2021). Performing Enclosures (Great Arenas Won't Lie Fallow). *OBLIO, Osservatorio Bibliografico della Letteratura Italiana dell'Otto-Novecento* XI, (42–43), 160–74.

Peet, R. & Watts, M., eds. (2004). *Liberation Ecologies: Environment, Development and Social Movements*. London: Routledge.

Pellizzoni, L. (2011). Governing through Disorder: Neoliberal Environmental Governance and Social Theory. *Global Environmental Change*, 21(3), 795–803.

Penone, G. (2009). *Writings 1968–2008*, edited by G. Maraniello & J. Watkins. Bologna: MAMbo.

Pinkus, K. (2010). Alchemical Mercury: A Theory of Ambivalence. Stanford, CA: Stanford University Press.

Pope Francis (2015). *Laudato sii*. Encyclical Letter, http://bit.ly/3t4xc0C.

Povinelli, E. A. (1995). Do Rocks Listen? The Cultural Politics of Apprehending Australian Aboriginal Labor. *American Anthropologist*, 97(3), 505–18.

  (2002). *The Cunning of Recognition: Indigenous Alterities and the Making of Australian Multiculturalism*. Durham, NC: Duke University Press.

  (2016). *Geontologies: A Requiem to Late Liberalism*. Durham, NC: Duke University Press.

  (2021). *Between Gaia and Ground: Four Axioms of Existence and the Ancestral Catastrophe of Late Liberalism*. Durham, NC: Duke University Press.

Proulx, G. & Crane, N. J. (2020). "To See Things in an Objective Light": The Dakota Access Pipeline and the Ongoing Construction of Settler Colonial Landscapes. *Journal of Cultural Geography*, 37(1), 46–66.

Prugh, T., Costanza, R., Cumberland, J. H., Daly, H., & Goodland, R. (1995). *Natural Capital and Human Economic Survival*. Boca Raton, FL: Lewis Publishers, CRC Press.

Quintana, L. (2020). *The Politics of Bodies: Philosophical Emancipation with and beyond Rancière*. Washington, DC: Rowman & Littlefield.

Raffles, H. (2020). *The Book of Unconformities: Speculations on Lost Time*. New York: Pantheon Books.

Rancière, J. (1992). Politics, Identification, and Subjectivization. *October*, 61, 58–64.

  (1999). *Disagreement: Politics and Philosophy*. Minneapolis: University of Minnesota Press.

Randerson, J. (2022). Serpents, Tsunami Boulders and Lightning. *Swamphen: A Journal of Cultural Ecology*, 8, https://doi.org/10.60162/swamphen.8.16687.

Reiter, B., ed. (2018). *Constructing the Pluriverse*. Durham, NC: Duke University Press.

Reynard, E. (2004). Protecting Stones: Conservation of Erratic Blocks in Switzerland. In R. Prikryl, ed., *Dimension Stone 2004 – New Perspectives for a Traditional Building Material*. London: Routledge.

Rights of Mother Earth (2010). *Universal Declaration of the Rights of Mother Earth*. From the World People's Conference on Climate Change and the Rights of Mother Earth, April 22, Cochabamba, Bolivia, https://bit.ly/46cThbA.

Riofrancos, T. (2020). *Resource Radicals: From Petro-Nationalism to Post-Extractivism in Ecuador*. Durham, NC: Duke University Press.

Rudwick, M. J. S. (2008). *Worlds before Adam: The Reconstruction of Geohistory in the Age of Reform*. Chicago, IL: University of Chicago Press.

Ryan, F. (2012). *Metamorphosis: Unmasking the Mystery of How Life Transforms*. London: Oneworld Publications.

Salmond, A. (2014). Tears of Rangi: Water, power, and people in New Zealand. *Hau: Journal of Ethnographic* Theory, 4(3), 285–309.

Sassen, S. (2013). Land Grabs Today: Feeding the Disassembling of National Territory. *Globalizations*, 10(1), 25–46.

Scott, A. (2011). Sacred Politics: An Examination of Inca Huacas and Their Use for Political and Social Organization. *The University of Western Ontario Journal of Anthropology*, 17(1), 23–36.

Seger, M. (2022). *Toxic Matters: Narrating Italy's Dioxin*. Charlottesville: University of Virginia Press.

Simondon, G. (2020). *Individuation in Light of Notions of Form and Information*. Minneapolis: University of Minnesota Press.

Smithson, R. (1979). *The Collected Writings*. Berkeley: University of California Press.

Spinoza, B. (2016). *The Collected Works of Spinoza*. Vol. II, edited by Edwin Curley. Princeton, NJ: Princeton University Press,

Steer, E. (2016). Interview: Julian Charrière. *Elephant Magazine*, April 27, www.skny.com/attachment/en/62f52bf90af321abff00fe82/Press/58d568a2ced750e17e938601.

Stone, C. D. (1972). Should Trees Have Standing? Towards Legal Rights for Natural Objects. *Southern California Law Review*, 45, 450–501.

(2010). *Should Trees Have Standing? Law, Morality, and the Environment*. Oxford: Oxford University Press.

Svampa, M. (2019). *Neo-extractivism in Latin America*. Cambridge: Cambridge University Press.

The White House (2023). Fact Sheet: President Biden to Catalyze Global Climate Action through the Major Economies Forum on Energy and Climate, April 20, https://bit.ly/45Ynbkf.

Theopfrastus (1956). *Theopfrastus on Stones*. Columbus: Ohio State University Press.

Thomas, Y. (1998). Le sujet de droit, le personne et la nature. *Le Débat*, 3(100), 85-107.

Tola, M. (2016). Composing with Gaia: Isabelle Stengers and the Feminist Politics of the Earth. *PhaenEx*, 11(1), 1–21.

(2018). Between Pachamama and Mother Earth: Gender, Political Ontology and the Rights of Nature in Contemporary Bolivia. *Feminist Review*, 118(1), 25–40.

Tsing, A. L. (2015). *The Mushroom at the End of the World: On the Possibility of Life in Capitalist Ruins*. Princeton, NJ: Princeton University Press.

Tsing, A. L., Swanson, H., Gan, E., & Bubandt, N. (2017). *Arts of Living on a Damaged Planet: Ghosts and Monsters of the Anthropocene*. Minneapolis: University of Minnesota Press.

Uhel, M. (2019). La "guerre de l'eau" à Cochabamba: De la réappropriation de l'espace politique à la reproduction d'un lieu symbolique de la contestation. *L'Espace Politique*, 37(1), http://journals.openedition.org/espacepolitique/6288.

Ulloa, A. (2017). The Geopolitics of Carbonized Nature and the Zero Carbon Citizen. *South Atlantic Quarterly*, 116(1), 111–20.

Vatter, M. E. & De Leeuw, M. (2019). Human Rights, Legal Personhood and the Impersonality of Embodied Life. Law, Culture and the Humanities, 1, UNSW Law Research Paper No. 85-19, https://dx.doi.org/10.2139/ssrn.3483310.

Velikovsky, I. (1955). *Earth in Upheaval*. New York: Doubleday.

Verweijen, J. & Dunlap, A. (2021). The Evolving Techniques of the Social Engineering of Extraction: Introducing Political (re)Actions "From above" in Large-scale Mining and Energy Projects. *Political Geography*, 88, www.sciencedirect.com/science/article/abs/pii/S0962629821000020.

Viveiros de Castro, E. (2004). Perspectival Anthropology and the Method of Controlled Equivocation. *Tipití: Journal of the Society for the Anthropology of Lowland South America*, 2(1), 3–22.

(2014). *Cannibal Metaphysics: For a Post-Structural Anthropology*. Minneapolis, MN: Univocal.

Wainwright, J. & Mann, G. (2018). *Climate Leviathan: A Political Theory of Our Planetary Future*. London: Verso.

Walker, J. & Cooper, M. (2011). Genealogies of Resilience: From Systems Ecology to the Political Economy of Crisis Adaptation. *Security Dialogue*, 42(2), 143–60.

Ward, B. & Dubos, R. (1972). *Only One Earth: The Care and Maintenance of a Small Planet*. New York: Norton.

Watson, J. E., Leiper, I., Potapov, P., et al. (2020). Importance of Indigenous Peoples' Lands for the Conservation of Intact Forest Landscapes. *Frontiers in Ecology and the Environment*, 18(3), 135–40.

Watts, M. (2015). Now and Then: The Origins of Political Ecology and the Rebirth of Adaptation as a Form of Thought. In T. Perreault, G. Bridge, & J. J. McCarthy, eds., *The Routledge Handbook of Political Ecology*. London: Routledge.

Whitcomb, J. C. & Morris, H. M. (1961). *The Genesis Flood: The Biblical Record and Its Scientific Implications*. Grand Rapids, MI: Baker Book House.

Winichakul, T. (1994). *Siam Mapped: A History of the Geo-Body of a Nation*. Honolulu: University of Hawaii Press.

Woodward, J. (2014). *The Ice Age: A Very Short Introduction*. Oxford: Oxford University Press.

Wynter, S. (1996). *1492: A New World View*. In V. Lawrence Hyatt and R. Nettleford, eds., *Race, Discourse and the Origins of the Americas*. Washington, DC: Smithsonian Institution Press.

(2015) *On Being Human as Praxis*. Durham, NC: Duke University Press.

Yoshida, H., Yamamoto, K., Minami, M., et al. (2018). Generalized Conditions of spherical Carbonate Concretion Formation around Decaying Organic Matter in Early Diagenesis. *Scientific Reports*, 8, 6308.

Yusoff, K. (2018). *A Billion Black Anthropocenes or None*. Minneapolis: University of Minnesota Press.

Zaragocin, S. & Caretta, M. A. (2021). *Cuerpo-Territorio*: A Decolonial Feminist Geographical Method for the Study of Embodiment. *Annals of the American Association of Geographers*, 111(5), 1–16.

Zucchelli, C. (2016). *Sacred Stones of Ireland*. Cork: The Collins Press.

Zumbach, C. (2019). Un nouveau quartier verra le jour à Onex. *Tribune de Genève*, September 18, www.tdg.ch/un-nouveau-quartier-verra-le-jour-a-onex-420823182057.

Cambridge Elements

Environmental Humanities

Louise Westling
University of Oregon

Louise Westling is an American scholar of literature and environmental humanities who was a founding member of the Association for the Study of Literature and Environment and its President in 1998. She has been active in the international movement for environmental cultural studies, teaching and writing on landscape imagery in literature, critical animal studies, biosemiotics, phenomenology, and deep history.

Serenella Iovino
University of North Carolina at Chapel Hill

Serenella Iovino is Professor of Italian Studies and Environmental Humanities at the University of North Carolina at Chapel Hill. She has written on a wide range of topics, including environmental ethics and ecocritical theory, bioregionalism and landscape studies, ecofeminism and posthumanism, comparative literature, eco-art, and the Anthropocene.

Timo Maran
University of Tartu

Timo Maran is an Estonian semiotician and poet. Maran is Professor of Ecosemiotics and Environmental Humanities and Head of the Department of Semiotics at the University of Tartu. His research interests are semiotic relations of nature and culture, Estonian nature writing, zoosemiotics and species conservation, and semiotics of biological mimicry.

About the Series

The environmental humanities is a new transdisciplinary complex of approaches to the embeddedness of human life and culture in all the dynamics that characterize the life of the planet. These approaches reexamine our species' history in light of the intensifying awareness of drastic climate change and ongoing mass extinction. To engage this reality, Cambridge Elements in Environmental Humanities builds on the idea of a more hybrid and participatory mode of research and debate, connecting critical and creative fields.

Cambridge Elements ≡

Environmental Humanities

Elements in the Series

A full series listing is available at: www.cambridge.org/EIEH

Printed in the United States
by Baker & Taylor Publisher Services